Chapel Talks

for Christian Children

2003–2004

Featuring 42 lessons on songs of the Bible

NORTHWESTERN PUBLISHING HOUSE

Milwaukee, Wisconsin

Northwestern Publishing House
1250 N. 113th St., Milwaukee, WI 53226-3284
www.nph.net
© 2003 by Northwestern Publishing House
Published 2003
Printed in the United States of America
ISBN 0-8100-1543-9

Preface

Chapel Talks for Christian Children is a resource for worship with children. It can be adapted to a variety of settings and applications, including Christian elementary schools, Sunday schools, vacation Bible schools, and children's sermons.

Each devotion has a leader's guide that includes
- the theme of the day
- a Bible text
- the suggested week for use
- suggestions for visual materials
- suggestions for an object lesson
- a Bible truth section for explaining and applying the text
- discussion and application questions

A copy master for each devotion includes
- a short order of service
- a song of praise for the season
- a text and prayer for the devotion
- a hymn for the day
- a psalm selection for the day
- optional prayers

Permission to copy the order of service is granted to purchasers of *Chapel Talks for Christian Children*. Such permission is not transferable to other congregations or institutions.

This series of 42 devotions is based on Bible texts that are familiar songs of God's people in the Bible as they proclaimed the wonderful things God had done for them. May the Lord of the church lead the children in your care to also praise and worship our God for his gracious works.

Carl S. Nolte
Editor

Acknowledgements

We gratefully acknowledge the dedicated writers of these lessons: Craig Charron, Aaron Christie, Steven Janke, and Jane Mose.

Table of Contents

At Home with Temptation
Psalm 1:1

Suggested for August 25–29, 2003

Visual Materials

- three volunteers
- four chairs

Object Lesson

Have the volunteers stand together near the chairs, pretending to talk with one another. Stand away from the group and ask: If I want to be a part of this group, what should I do? Should I walk over and say hello?

Stand with the volunteers, and briefly pretend to join in their conversation. Point out that after standing with them and getting to know them, you might become friends. Have the volunteers sit in the chairs; join them. Suggest that perhaps you could all go out to eat, see a movie, or spend time together at someone's house, when you feel truly comfortable with them.

Bible Truth

Psalm 1:1 says, **"Blessed is the man who does not walk in the counsel of the wicked or stand in the way of sinners or sit in the seat of mockers."**

Explain that this year the children will learn from songs that are found in the Bible. Today's song is from the book of Psalms, which was the hymnal of God's people long ago. The first verse of the first song refers to *walking* with the wicked, *standing* with sinners, and *sitting* with mockers. Ask: What might happen if we walk with wicked people, such as by listening to their advice? What might happen if we stand with sinners who don't love God by hanging around with them? What if we sit with people who mock—make fun of—God's ways by making ourselves at home with them?

Point out that the world is full of temptations to sin, especially from people who don't love God. If we don't avoid these temptations, they'll not only walk into our lives but also stand firmly planted there and even sit down and make themselves at home with us! But, thankfully, we have the Holy Spirit on our side to help us resist temptation. And when we give in to temptation, we have the forgiveness Jesus won for us by his death on the cross. Let's thank Jesus for his goodness by avoiding temptations with the Spirit's help.

Discussions and Applications

1. How might watching TV programs or videos that show sinful activities be like walking, standing, or sitting with the wicked?

2. What will you want to consider when choosing your closest friends?

CHAPEL TALKS FOR CHRISTIAN CHILDREN

AUGUST 25–29, 2003

Leader: As children of God, we worship the Lord our Savior.

Children: Let us unite our hearts and voices to praise his holy name.

SONG OF PRAISE Lord, Open Now My Heart to Hear*

Geistliche Lieder zu Wittemberg

Johannes Olearius
tr. Matthias Loy, st. 1,3
Mark A. Jeske, st. 2

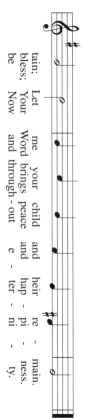
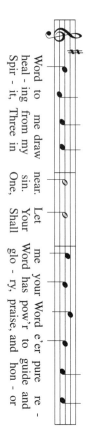

1. Lord, o - pen now my heart to hear, And through your
2. Your Word in - spires my heart with - in; Your Word grants
3. To God the Fa - ther, God the Son, And God the

Word to me draw near. Let me your Word e'er pure re -
heal - ing from my sin. Your Word has pow'r to guide and
Spir - it, Three in One, Shall glo - ry, praise, and hon - or

tain; Let me your child and heir re - main.
bless; Your Word brings peace and hap - pi - ness.
be Now and through - out e - ter - ni - ty.

Leader: Holy Spirit, the world is full of people trying to make us feel at home with sin and its temptations. It is too easy for us to get comfortable with sinful words and activities. Teach us to recognize these dangers and avoid them. Strengthen us, and help us resist all the temptations around us. We pray this in Jesus' name. Amen.

THE MESSAGE At Home with Temptation

Blessed is the man who does not walk in the counsel of the wicked or stand in the way of sinners or sit in the seat of mockers (Psalm 1:1).

HYMN The Man Is Ever Blest

The man is ever blest
Who shuns the sinners' ways,
Among their counsels never stands,
Nor takes the scorners' place,

But makes the law of God
His study and delight
Amid the labors of the day
And watches of the night.

God knows and he approves
The way the righteous go,
But sinners and their works shall meet
A dreadful overthrow.

PSALM 1

Leader: Blessed is the man who does not walk in the counsel of the wicked

Children: Or stand in the way of sinners or sit in the seat of mockers.

Leader: But his delight is in the law of the LORD,

Children: And on his law he meditates day and night.

Leader: He is like a tree planted by streams of water,

Children: Which yields its fruit in season

Leader: And whose leaf does not wither.

Children: Whatever he does prospers.

PRAYER REQUESTS

THE LORD'S PRAYER (*spoken together*)

OFFERINGS OF LOVE FOR JESUS

Leader: Now, children, go in peace. Live in harmony with one another. Serve the Lord with gladness.

The grace of our Lord + Jesus Christ and the love of God and the fellowship of the Holy Spirit be with you all.

Children: Amen.

Time with the Word
Psalm 1:2

Suggested for September 1–5, 2003

Visual Materials

- a grid of 168 squares or rectangles (for example, 12 x 14 rows)
- two markers, one yellow and one blue
- a Bible

Object Lesson

Show the grid. Point out that it has 168 spaces, the same number as there are hours in a week. Ask the children to think of a favorite activity—something they love to do. Ask: How many hours a week would you like to spend on that activity? How many more hours might you spend just thinking about that activity? Use the yellow marker to roughly fill in the correct number of spaces.

Tell the children that today's Bible passage will talk about the time we spend with "the law of the LORD." Show the Bible, and explain that in this passage, "the law of the LORD" refers to all of God's Word, both law and gospel.

Bible Truth

Psalm 1:2 says, **"His delight is in the law of the LORD, and on his law he meditates day and night."**

Explain that today the group will continue to look at the biblical song of Psalm 1. Last week's passage talked about a person being blessed when he avoids temptation. Today, that same blessed person is described as finding delight—great enjoyment—in God's Word. The blessed person is also described as someone who meditates on, or thinks about, God's Word day and night.

Ask: How many hours each week do you usually spend in church? in Sunday school? (if applicable) in Word of God class in our Lutheran elementary school? Use the blue marker to fill in the appropriate number of spaces on your grid. Remind the children that the world is full of temptations. The Holy Spirit uses God's Word to strengthen us and help us resist those temptations. But we cannot expect to have the strength to resist those temptations if we only think about God's Word a few hours out of the 168 in each week. It is important to spend as much time as possible reading and learning God's Word and then remembering and thinking about God's truths throughout every day. The Holy Spirit will use this time with the Word not only to strengthen us but also to give us the joy that comes from hearing God's wonderful messages of love.

Discussions and Applications

1. When could you add more time with God's Word into your busy days?

2. What are some of the messages in God's Word that bring you great joy?

CHAPEL TALKS FOR CHRISTIAN CHILDREN
SEPTEMBER 1–5, 2003

Leader: As children of God, we worship the Lord our Savior.

Children: Let us unite our hearts and voices to praise his holy name.

SONG OF PRAISE Lord, Open Now My Heart to Hear*

Johannes Olearius
tr. Matthias Loy, st. 1,3
Mark A. Jeske, st. 2

Geistliche Lieder zu Wittemberg

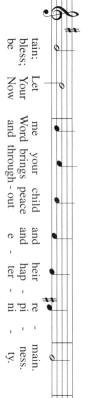

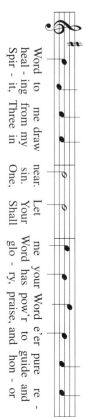

1. Lord, o - pen now my heart to hear, And through your
2. Your Word in - spires my heart with - in; Your Word grants
3. To God the Fa - ther, God the Son, And God the

Word to me draw near. Let me your Word e'er pure re -
heal - ing from my sin. Your Word has pow'r to guide and
Spir - it, Three in One, Shall glo - ry, praise, and hon - or

tain; Let me your child and heir re - main.
bless; Your Word brings peace and hap - pi - ness.
be Now and through - out e - ter - ni - ty.

THE MESSAGE Time with the Word

His delight is in the law of the LORD, and on his law he meditates day and night (Psalm 1:2).

Leader: Dear God, we thank you for the wonderful messages in your Word—especially for the message that we are saved through faith in Jesus. Teach us to see that time learning your Word is very important. Lead us to experience the joy of thinking about your Word day and night. Amen.

*Text tr. st. 2: © Mark A. Jeske. Used by permission.

HYMN Lord, Keep Us Steadfast in Your Word

Lord, keep us steadfast in your Word;
Curb those who by deceit or sword
Would seek to overthrow your Son
And to destroy what he has done.

Lord Jesus Christ, your pow'r make known,
For you are Lord of lords alone;
Defend your Christendom that we
May sing your praise eternally.

O Comforter of priceless worth,
Send peace and unity on earth.
Support us in our final strife,
And lead us out of death to life.

PSALM 119

Leader: Oh, how I love your law!

Children: I meditate on it all day long.

Leader: Your commands make me wiser than my enemies,

Children: For they are ever with me.

Leader: I have more insight than all my teachers,

Children: For I meditate on your statutes.

PRAYER REQUESTS

THE LORD'S PRAYER *(spoken together)*

OFFERINGS OF LOVE FOR JESUS

Leader: Now, children, go in peace. Live in harmony with one another. Serve the Lord with gladness. The grace of our Lord ✝ Jesus Christ and the love of God and the fellowship of the Holy Spirit be with you all.

Children: Amen.

Well-Watered Trees
Psalm 1:3

Suggested for September 8–12, 2003

Visual Materials

- two drawings, one of a healthy, leafy tree and another of a sickly tree with only a few withered leaves (Optional: Draw a tree trunk with branches on each side. Tape healthy, green leaves from a real tree on one side but withered leaves on the other side.)
- an apple

Object Lesson

Show the drawing of the healthy tree. Tell the children to pretend it is an apple tree. Ask: What would this tree need to grow well? If it has a good place to grow with plenty of water, what will we find on it in the fall? Show the apple. But what will happen to it if it gets no water? Show the withered tree, pointing out that it will not produce any fruit.

Bible Truth

Explain that the group will continue to look at the Bible song found in Psalm 1. **Psalm 1:3** continues to talk about a blessed man, saying: **"He is like a tree planted by streams of water, which yields its fruit in season and whose leaf does not wither. Whatever he does prospers."**

Remind the children that last week the group talked about the joy Christians have in learning God's Word. Ask: What messages in God's Word bring you the greatest joy? Explain that Christians are like trees. When they are motivated by the Bible's gospel message, they produce fruits of faith. These fruits are good works—actions that are done out of love for God. But in order to be healthy trees that produce fruits of faith, we need to be well watered. We are "watered" by God's Word. The Holy Spirit uses God's Word to strengthen our faith, keep it healthy, and make it able to produce good fruits. Without the water of God's Word, our faith withers away. Encourage the children to "water their trees" often by hearing and reading God's Word and to produce fruits of faith by showing their love for God in all they do.

Discussions and Applications

1. What are some fruits of faith that children your age can do?

2. When you're finding it hard to produce fruits of faith, what can you do?

CHAPEL TALKS FOR CHRISTIAN CHILDREN
SEPTEMBER 8–12, 2003

Leader: As children of God, we worship the Lord our Savior.

Children: **Let us unite our hearts and voices to praise his holy name.**

SONG OF PRAISE Lord, Open Now My Heart to Hear*

Johannes Olearius
tr. Matthias Loy, st. 1,3
Mark A. Jeske, st. 2

Geistliche Lieder zu Wittemberg

1. Lord, o - pen now my heart to hear, And through your
2. Your Word in - spires my heart with - in; Your Word grants
3. To God the Fa - ther, God the Son, And God the

Word to me draw near. Let me your Word e'er pure re -
heal - ing from my sin. Your Word has pow'r to guide and
Spir - it, Three in One, Shall glo - ry, praise, and hon - or

tain; Let me your child and heir re - main.
bless; Your Word brings peace and hap - pi - ness.
be Now and through - out e - ter - ni - ty.

THE MESSAGE Well-Watered Trees

He is like a tree planted by streams of water, which yields its fruit in season and whose leaf does not wither. Whatever he does prospers (Psalm 1:3).

Leader: Heavenly Father, thank you for the gift of your Word, which waters our souls every time we hear and learn it. Thank you also for sending your Son to take away our sins. We want to show our thankfulness to you by producing fruits of faith. Through your Holy Spirit, strengthen our faith, and keep us well-watered trees throughout our lives. We pray in Jesus' name. Amen.

HYMN The Man Is Ever Blest

The man is ever blest
Who shuns the sinners' ways,
Among their counsels never stands,
Nor takes the scorners' place,

He like a tree shall thrive
With waters near the root.
Fresh as the leaf his name shall live;
His works are heav'nly fruit.

God knows and he approves
The way the righteous go,
But sinners and their works shall meet
A dreadful overthrow.

PSALM 119

Leader: Blessed are they whose ways are blameless,

Children: **Who walk according to the law of the LORD.**

Leader: Blessed are they who keep his statutes

Children: **And seek him with all their heart.**

Leader: They do nothing wrong;

Children: **They walk in his ways.**

PRAYER REQUESTS

THE LORD'S PRAYER (*spoken together*)

OFFERINGS OF LOVE FOR JESUS

Leader: Now, children, go in peace. Live in harmony with one another. Serve the Lord with gladness.

The grace of our Lord ✝ Jesus Christ and the love of God and the fellowship of the Holy Spirit be with you all.

Children: **Amen.**

Grain or Chaff
Psalm 1:4-6

Suggested for September 15–19, 2003

Visual Materials

- a small bowl of potato flakes and white rice mixed together
- a 9" x 13" cake pan
- a dropcloth or vacuum for quick cleanup (optional)

Object Lesson

Explain that in Bible times farmers didn't have farm machines called combines that we have today to help separate the good parts of a harvested plant from the worthless parts. In Bible times farmers separated good grain from worthless chaff by using the wind.

Show the bowl of potato flakes and rice, pointing out how time consuming it could be to separate the two. Then hold the cake pan chest high in front of you, and grab a handful of the flakes and rice. Throw the mixture up in front of your face, and blow hard on it so that the rice drops into the cake pan and the potato flakes go past the pan, dropping onto the floor or dropcloth. Show the results. Explain that this happened because the flakes are lighter than the rice and easier to blow away. In the same way, chaff was lighter than grain. Farmers would throw the grain-chaff mixture into the air on a windy day, letting the wind blow away the chaff while the grain landed in a pile on the ground.

Bible Truth

Explain that today the group will finish looking at the Bible song of Psalm 1. After talking about how the believer is blessed, **Psalm 1:4-6** says: **"Not so the wicked! They are like chaff that the wind blows away. Therefore the wicked will not stand in the judgment, nor sinners in the assembly of the righteous. For the LORD watches over the way of the righteous, but the way of the wicked will perish."**

God tells us that on judgment day he will gather believers into their home in heaven just as a farmer gathers good grain into his barn. But unbelievers will be blown away from God's presence like chaff in the wind.

This is why it is dangerous to even begin to follow the ways of unbelievers. We don't want to be led away from our Savior and the road to heaven. Instead, we want to be "well watered" with God's Word so that our faith in Jesus remains strong. All who have been given the gift of faith in Jesus as their Savior can trust that they will not be "blown away" from God but gathered into their heavenly home.

Discussions and Applications

1. Why are we saddened when we think of all the unbelievers in the world?

2. Why are we sure that we will live in heaven?

CHAPEL TALKS FOR CHRISTIAN CHILDREN
SEPTEMBER 15–19, 2003

Leader: As children of God, we worship the Lord our Savior.

Children: **Let us unite our hearts and voices to praise his holy name.**

SONG OF PRAISE Lord, Open Now My Heart to Hear*

Geistliche Lieder zu Wittemberg

Johannes Olearius
tr. Matthias Loy, st. 1,3
Mark A. Jeske, st. 2

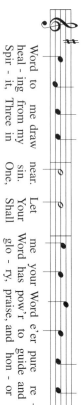

1. Lord, o - pen now my heart to hear, And through your
2. Your Word in - spires my heart with - in; Your Word grants
3. To God the Fa - ther, God the Son, And God the

Word to me draw near. Let me your Word e'er pure re -
heal - ing from my sin. Your Word has pow'r to guide and
Spir - it, Three in One, Shall glo - ry, praise, and hon - or

tain; Let me your child and heir re - main.
bless; Your Word brings peace and hap - pi - ness.
be Now and through - out e - ter - ni - ty.

THE MESSAGE Grain or Chaff

Not so the wicked! They are like chaff that the wind blows away. Therefore the wicked will not stand in the judgment, nor sinners in the assembly of the righteous. For the LORD watches over the way of the righteous, but the way of the wicked will perish (Psalm 1:4-6).

Leader: Dear Holy Spirit, thank you for the gift of faith in Jesus our Savior. Help us resist this world's temptations so that we never reject our Savior. Keep us faithful Christians until we reach our heavenly home. Amen.

HYMN Draw Us to Thee

Draw us to thee, For then shall we
Walk in thy steps forever
And hasten on Where thou art gone
To be with thee, dear Savior.

Draw us to thee; Oh, grant that we
May walk the road to heaven!
Direct our way Lest we should stray
And from thy paths be driven.

Draw us to thee Unceasingly;
Into thy kingdom take us.
Let us fore'er Thy glory share;
Thy saints and joint heirs make us.

PSALM 1

Leader: Blessed is the man who does not walk in the counsel of the wicked

Children: **Or stand in the way of sinners or sit in the seat of mockers.**

Leader: The wicked will not stand in the judgment,

Children: **Nor sinners in the assembly of the righteous.**

Leader: For the LORD watches over the way of the righteous,

Children: **But the way of the wicked will perish.**

PRAYER REQUESTS

THE LORD'S PRAYER *(spoken together)*

OFFERINGS OF LOVE FOR JESUS

Leader: Now, children, go in peace. Live in harmony with one another. Serve the Lord with gladness.

The grace of our Lord ☩ Jesus Christ and the love of God and the fellowship of the Holy Spirit be with you all.

Children: **Amen.**

Praise Everywhere
Psalm 150:1,2

5

Suggested for September 22–26, 2003

Visual Materials

- the church sanctuary (have this devotion in your church sanctuary if possible) or a picture of the inside of a church

Object Lesson

Ask: Whose house are we in? What are some things in this church that remind you that it is God's house? What do we do in this special place? Explain that the part of God's house in which we worship him is called the sanctuary.

Bible Truth

Tell the children that today they will begin looking at another Bible song, Psalm 150. **Psalm 150:1,2** says: **"Praise the Lord. Praise God in his sanctuary; praise him in his mighty heavens. Praise him for his acts of power; praise him for his surpassing greatness."**

This psalm tells us where to praise God: now in his sanctuary on earth and someday also in heaven. In other words, we are to praise him everywhere! Ask: What are some ways we praise God here in church?

The psalm also tells us to praise God for his acts of power and for his greatness. Ask: What are some ways God showed his power and greatness in the Bible? How does he still show his power and greatness today? Point out the most wonderful way God has shown his power—by sending Jesus to defeat the devil's power and win forgiveness for our sins. Encourage the children to look for opportunities to praise God for his power and greatness everywhere here on earth until someday they can praise him in heaven.

Discussions and Applications

1. Why do you want to praise God?

2. Where are some other places, besides this sanctuary, that you can praise God?

CHAPEL TALKS FOR CHRISTIAN CHILDREN
SEPTEMBER 22–26, 2003

Leader: As children of God, we worship the Lord our Savior.

Children: Let us unite our hearts and voices to praise his holy name.

SONG OF PRAISE Rejoice in the Lord Always

Philippians 4:4

Anonymous

Re - joice in the Lord al - ways; a -

gain I say re - joice. Re - joice in the Lord

al - ways; a - gain I say re - joice. Re -

joice, re - joice; a - gain I say re - joice. Re -

joice, re - joice; a - gain I say re - joice.

Leader: Dear God, we want to praise you for your incredible power and greatness, especially in sending Jesus to win victory over the devil for us. You are truly an awesome God! Lead us to praise you everywhere we can here on earth until we have the joy of praising you in heaven. Amen.

HYMN Lord Jesus Christ, Be Present Now

Lord Jesus Christ, be present now;
Our hearts in true devotion bow.
Your Spirit send with grace divine,
And let your truth within us shine.

Unseal our lips to sing your praise;
Our souls to you in worship raise.
Make strong our faith; increase our light
That we may know your name aright.

Glory to God the Father, Son,
And Holy Spirit, Three in One!
To you, O blessed Trinity,
Be praise throughout eternity!

PSALM 148

Leader: Praise the LORD. Praise the LORD from the heavens,

Children: Praise him in the heights above.

Leader: Praise him, all his angels,

Children: Praise him, all his heavenly hosts.

Leader: Praise him, sun and moon,

Children: Praise him, all you shining stars.

Leader: Praise him, you highest heavens

Children: And you waters above the skies.

PRAYER REQUESTS

THE LORD'S PRAYER (spoken together)

OFFERINGS OF LOVE FOR JESUS

Leader: Now, children, go in peace. Live in harmony with one another. Serve the Lord with gladness.

The grace of our Lord ✠ Jesus Christ and the love of God and the fellowship of the Holy Spirit be with you all.

Children: Amen.

THE MESSAGE Praise Everywhere

Praise the LORD. Praise God in his sanctuary; praise him in his mighty heavens. Praise him for his acts of power; praise him for his surpassing greatness (Psalm 150:1,2).

Joyful Praise
Psalm 150:3-5

Suggested for September 29–October 3, 2003

Visual Materials

- some of the instruments mentioned in the psalm (harp, lyre, tambourine, string instruments, flute, cymbals)
- (optional) rhythm band instruments

Object Lesson

Tell the children that some instruments are named in today's Bible. Show some of the instruments mentioned in the psalm, and help the children identify each. Ask the children to name some of the instruments they may have learned to play. Point out that even if the children haven't had formal lessons on certain instruments, there are some instruments they can all play, such as rhythm band instruments. If time allows, hand out some rhythm band instruments, and let the children make joyful rhythm sounds while singing a familiar song of praise, such as "Praise Him, Praise Him" or "My God Is So Great." Point out that a singing voice is also considered a musical instrument for praise.

Bible Truth

Explain that the group will continue to look at the Bible song in Psalm 150. **Psalm 150:3-5** says, **"Praise him with the sounding of the trumpet, praise him with the harp and lyre, praise him with tambourine and dancing, praise him with the strings and flute, praise him with the clash of cymbals, praise him with resounding cymbals."**

This psalm names a number of instruments that can be used to praise God. Ask: Do you think these are the *only* instruments we are to use to praise God? What other instruments can we use? Explain that God wants us to praise him joyfully with everything we have—all instruments and our voices as well. We praise God especially for his gift of salvation through Jesus. Encourage the children to praise God enthusiastically and joyfully with everything they have!

Discussions and Applications

1. What kinds of musical instruments can be used to praise God?

2. What can you do if you want to praise God joyfully but don't think you're good with music?

CHAPEL TALKS FOR CHRISTIAN CHILDREN
SEPTEMBER 29–OCTOBER 3, 2003

Leader: As children of God, we worship the Lord our Savior.

Children: **Let us unite our hearts and voices to praise his holy name.**

SONG OF PRAISE Rejoice in the Lord Always

Philippians 4:4

Anonymous

Re - joice in the Lord___ al - ways; a -

gain I say re - joice. Re - joice in the Lord___

al - ways; a - gain I say re - joice. Re -

joice, re - joice; a - gain I say re - joice. Re -

joice, re - joice; a - gain I say re - joice.

Leader: Dear God, thank you for your amazing goodness to us! We want to praise you with everything we have. Help us to not be shy or weak in our praise. Instead, lead us to show our thankfulness to you with joyful and enthusiastic songs of praise. We pray in Jesus' name. Amen.

HYMN All Praise To God Who Reigns Above

All praise to God who reigns above,
The God of all creation,
The God of wonders, pow'r, and love,
The God of our salvation!
With healing balm my soul he fills,
The God who ev'ry sorrow stills—
To God all praise and glory!

All who confess Christ's holy name,
To God give praise and glory!
All who the Father's pow'r proclaim,
To God give praise and glory!
All idols under foot be trod;
The Lord is God! The Lord is God!
To God all praise and glory!

PSALM 150

Leader: Praise God in his sanctuary;

Children: **Praise him in his mighty heavens.**

Leader: Praise him with the sounding of the trumpet,

Children: **Praise him with the harp and lyre,**

Leader: Praise him with tambourine and dancing,

Children: **Praise him with the strings and flute,**

Leader: Praise him with the clash of cymbals,

Children: **Praise him with resounding cymbals.**

PRAYER REQUESTS

THE LORD'S PRAYER (*spoken together*)

OFFERINGS OF LOVE FOR JESUS

Leader: Now, children, go in peace. Live in harmony with one another. Serve the Lord with gladness.

The grace of our Lord ✝ Jesus Christ and the love of God and the fellowship of the Holy Spirit be with you all.

Children: **Amen.**

THE MESSAGE Joyful Praise

Praise him with the sounding of the trumpet, praise him with the harp and lyre, praise him with tambourine and dancing, praise him with the strings and flute, praise him with the clash of cymbals, praise him with resounding cymbals (Psalm 150:3-5).

Everything That Has Breath
Psalm 150:6

Suggested for October 6–10, 2003

Visual Materials

- a mirror

Object Lesson

Ask: How many of you have breath in your body? How do you know? Can you see your breath? Give several children the opportunity to "see" their breath by breathing onto the mirror. Establish that every living person has breath. Tell the children that today's Bible passage has a command for "everything that has breath."

Bible Truth

Explain that today the group will examine the conclusion of **Psalm 150.** The last verse of this song, **verse 6,** says: **"Let everything that has breath praise the LORD. Praise the LORD."**

Ask: What does this passage tell "everything that has breath" to do? Why do we praise the Lord? Point out that the children can praise the Lord in many ways—not only with songs and prayers but also by serving the Lord in every way they can out of love for him.

Ask: Why are we able to praise the Lord? Since God has given us the gift of faith and the ability to praise him, it is our joy and privilege to be able to do so. As long as we have breath, let's praise God in every way we can!

Discussions and Applications

1. Why is it a privilege to be able to praise the Lord?

2. What are some ways you can praise the Lord in your everyday life?

CHAPEL TALKS FOR CHRISTIAN CHILDREN
OCTOBER 6–10, 2003

Leader: As children of God, we worship the Lord our Savior.

Children: **Let us unite our hearts and voices to praise his holy name.**

SONG OF PRAISE   Rejoice in the Lord Always

Philippians 4:4

Anonymous

Re - joice in the Lord al - ways; a - gain I say re - joice. Re - joice in the Lord al - ways; a - gain I say re - joice. Re - joice, re - joice; a - gain I say re - joice. Re - joice, re - joice; a - gain I say re - joice.

Leader: Lord God, thank you for giving us the privilege of being able to praise you. We are sorry for the times we haven't appreciated this wonderful privilege. Make us more eager to praise you joyfully for all your goodness. Amen.

HYMN   Praise to the Lord, the Almighty

Praise to the Lord, the Almighty, the King of creation!
O my soul, praise him, for he is your health and salvation!
Let all who hear Now to his temple draw near,
Joining in glad adoration!

Praise to the Lord! Oh, let all that is in me adore him!
All that has life and breath, come now with praises before him!
Let the Amen Sound from his people again;
Gladly forever adore him!

PSALM 150

Leader: Praise the LORD.

Children: **Praise him in his mighty heavens.**

Leader: Praise him for his acts of power;

Children: **Praise him for his surpassing greatness.**

Leader: Let everything that has breath praise the LORD.

Children: **Praise the LORD.**

PRAYER REQUESTS

THE LORD'S PRAYER (*spoken together*)

OFFERINGS OF LOVE FOR JESUS

Leader: Now, children, go in peace. Live in harmony with one another. Serve the Lord with gladness.

The grace of our Lord ✝ Jesus Christ and the love of God and the fellowship of the Holy Spirit be with you all.

Children: **Amen.**

THE MESSAGE   Everything That Has Breath

Let everything that has breath praise the LORD. Praise the LORD (Psalm 150:6).

Worship the Rock
Psalm 95:1,2

Suggested for October 13–17, 2003

Visual Materials

- clay (or Play-Doh or another easily malleable substance)
- a solid rock

Object Lesson

Show the clay, and ask a child to show what can be done with it. Point out that it is easy to change the clay by pulling it apart, twisting it into different shapes, and the like. Then hand the child the rock. Ask the child to change the rock in the same way.

Mention that today's Bible passage calls the Lord a "Rock." Encourage the children to think about why we can compare the Lord to a rock.

Bible Truth

Explain that today the group will begin looking at another song from the Bible, Psalm 95. **Psalm 95:1,2** says: **"Come, let us sing for joy to the LORD; let us shout aloud to the Rock of our salvation. Let us come before him with thanksgiving and extol him with music and song."**

Ask: In what way can we compare the Lord to a rock? The Lord stays the same; he's unchanging. The Lord is called "the Rock of our salvation." *Salvation* refers to the fact that we are saved through Jesus. Wouldn't it be awful if the Lord were to change his mind about our salvation—if he were to decide that Jesus' sacrifice for us is no longer enough, and we will be punished in hell for our sins? But the Lord won't change his mind, because he is unchanging. He will keep all his promises.

For this reason, the psalmist tells us to "sing for joy," "shout aloud," "come . . . with thanksgiving," and "extol [praise] [the Lord] with music and song." Jesus died for us. We have salvation through him. Let's worship the Lord with joy!

Discussions and Applications

1. Why are you thankful that the Lord never changes?

2. How can we show our joy when we worship?

CHAPEL TALKS FOR CHRISTIAN CHILDREN
OCTOBER 13–17, 2003

Leader: As children of God, we worship the Lord our Savior.

Children: **Let us unite our hearts and voices to praise his holy name.**

SONG OF PRAISE Rejoice in the Lord Always

Philippians 4:4

Anonymous

① Re - joice in the Lord ② al - ways; a -

gain I say re - joice. Re - joice in the Lord ③ Re -

al - ways; a - gain I say re - joice. ④ Re -

joice, re - joice; a - gain I say re - joice.

joice, re - joice; a - gain I say re - joice.

joice, re - joice; a - gain I say re - joice.

THE MESSAGE Worship the Rock

Leader: *Come, let us sing for joy to the LORD; let us shout aloud to the Rock of our salvation. Let us come before him with thanksgiving and extol him with music and song (Psalm 95:1,2).*

Leader: Lord God, Rock of our salvation, we praise you for your unchanging goodness. How thankful we are that we can

trust in all your promises to us! Let us always come before you with thanksgiving, singing for joy to you all our days. Amen.

HYMN Come, Let Us Join Our Cheerful Songs

Come, let us join our cheerful songs
With angels round the throne.
Ten thousand thousand are their tongues,
But all their joys are one.

"Worthy the Lamb that died," they cry,
"To be exalted thus."
"Worthy the Lamb," our lips reply,
"For he was slain for us."

Jesus is worthy to receive
Honor and pow'r divine;
And blessings more than we can give
Be, Lord, forever thine.

Let all creation join in one
To bless the sacred name
Of him who sits upon the throne
And to adore the Lamb.

PSALM 18

Leader: The LORD is my rock,

Children: **My fortress and my deliverer;**

Leader: My God is my rock,

Children: **In whom I take refuge.**

Leader: He is my shield

Children: **And the horn of my salvation, my stronghold.**

PRAYER REQUESTS

THE LORD'S PRAYER (*spoken together*)

OFFERINGS OF LOVE FOR JESUS

Leader: Now, children, go in peace. Live in harmony with one another. Serve the Lord with gladness. The grace of our Lord ✛ Jesus Christ and the love of God and the fellowship of the Holy Spirit be with you all.

Children: **Amen.**

Honor the King
Psalm 95:3-7

Suggested for October 20–24, 2003

Visual Materials

- a paper crown

Object Lesson

Put the crown on a boy's head. Ask the other children: Who usually wears a crown? Since he has a crown on his head, is he a real king now? Point out that a person doesn't get to be a king simply because he puts a crown on his head. There are certain qualifications for becoming a king.

Make the point that today's Bible passage refers to the Lord as "the great King above all gods"—the King over everyone and everything. The group will find out why the Lord is King over all.

Bible Truth

Explain that today the group will finish looking at **Psalm 95.** Verses **3-7** of this psalm say: **"The LORD is the great God, the great King above all gods. In his hand are the depths of the earth, and the mountain peaks belong to him. The sea is his, for he made it, and his hands formed the dry land. Come, let us bow down in worship, let us kneel before the LORD our Maker; for he is our God and we are the people of his pasture, the flock under his care."**

The psalm says that the deepest parts of the earth are in the Lord's hand, the mountain peaks belong to him, and the sea is his. Ask: Why is God the ruler, or King, over all parts of this world? God is King over all because he made everything. He made us too, and he is our King. Ask: Is God a harsh, cruel King? In verse 7 we read that "we are the people of his pasture, the flock under his care." Our King loves and cares for us as a shepherd loves and cares for his sheep. Ask: What is the most loving thing that God did for us so that we could be his people, members of his kingdom?

Because God made us, cares for us, and especially because he has saved us, we are invited to "bow down in worship" and "kneel before the LORD our Maker." Encourage the children to honor and worship the Lord, their King.

Discussions and Applications

1. Why are you glad to know that God is ruling over everyone and everything in the world?

2. How can you "bow down" to the Lord and "kneel before" him when you can't see him?

CHAPEL TALKS FOR CHRISTIAN CHILDREN
OCTOBER 20–24, 2003

Leader: As children of God, we worship the Lord our Savior.

Children: **Let us unite our hearts and voices to praise his holy name.**

SONG OF PRAISE Rejoice in the Lord Always

Philippians 4:4

Anonymous

Re - joice in the Lord al - ways; a -

gain I say re - joice. Re - joice in the Lord

al - ways; a - gain I say re - joice. Re -

joice, re - joice; a - gain I say re - joice. Re -

joice, re - joice; a - gain I say re - joice.

THE MESSAGE Honor the King

The LORD is the great God, the great King above all gods. In his hand are the depths of the earth, and the mountain peaks belong to him. The sea is his, for he made it, and his hands formed the dry land. Come, let us bow down in worship, let us kneel before the LORD our Maker; for he is our God and we are the people of his pasture, the flock under his care (Psalm 95:3-7).

Leader: Heavenly King, you truly deserve all honor and adora-tion. We praise you for your wonderful work of creation. We thank you for taking care of all our needs. Most of all, we worship you for your gift of salvation. Keep us faithful to you so that we may be members of your kingdom forever. Amen.

HYMN Beautiful Savior

Beautiful Savior, King of creation,
Son of God and Son of Man!
Truly I'd love thee, Truly I'd serve thee,
Light of my soul, my Joy, my Crown.

Beautiful Savior, Lord of the nations,
Son of God and Son of Man!
Glory and honor, Praise, adoration
Now and forevermore be thine!

PSALM 95

Leader: Come, let us bow down in worship,

Children: **Let us kneel before the LORD our Maker;**

Leader: For the LORD is the great God,

Children: **The great King above all gods.**

Leader: For he is our God and we are the people of his pasture,

Children: **The flock under his care.**

PRAYER REQUESTS

THE LORD'S PRAYER (*spoken together*)

OFFERINGS OF LOVE FOR JESUS

Leader: Now, children, go in peace. Live in harmony with one another. Serve the Lord with gladness.

The grace of our Lord ✝ Jesus Christ and the love of God and the fellowship of the Holy Spirit be with you all.

Children: **Amen.**

Our Refuge
Psalm 46:1-3

Suggested for October 27–31, 2003

Visual Materials

- toy animals, such as a turtle, mouse, or cat
- a baby doll

Object Lesson

Explain that many animals have places where they go to be safe when enemies are after them. Such a place of safety is a refuge for an animal. Hold up each toy animal, and ask where that animal might go for refuge, such as a turtle going inside its shell, a mouse running into a mousehole, and a cat climbing up a tree. Then show the baby doll and ask: Where does a little child go to feel safe? Point out that a parent's arms can be a refuge. Tell the group that today it will hear who the almighty refuge is.

Bible Truth

Tell the children that today they will begin reading another Bible song, Psalm 46. **Psalm 46:1-3** says: **"God is our refuge and strength, an ever-present help in trouble. Therefore we will not fear, though the earth give way and the mountains fall into the heart of the sea, though its waters roar and foam and the mountains quake with their surging."**

Ask: Who is our refuge? How is God a refuge? Point out that the psalm calls him an "ever-present help in trouble"—a refuge who is always with us, protecting us. Because of this, we don't need to be afraid, even when we have troubles as great as a mountain collapsing into the sea or an enormous earthquake. God is more powerful than any trouble that may come, and he is ready to help us.

Remind the children that God has already provided us with protection from our worst enemy, the devil. He did this through Jesus' suffering, death, and resurrection, which defeated the devil. Our God, who loves us so much that he sent his Son to die for us, will surely provide refuge from all our troubles.

Discussions and Applications

1. What are some troubles that can make us fearful?

2. What can we do when we need God's refuge and strength?

CHAPEL TALKS FOR CHRISTIAN CHILDREN
OCTOBER 27–31, 2003

Leader: As children of God, we worship the Lord our Savior.

Children: **Let us unite our hearts and voices to praise his holy name.**

SONG OF PRAISE Praise God, from Whom All Blessings Flow

Thomas Ken   Thomas Tallis

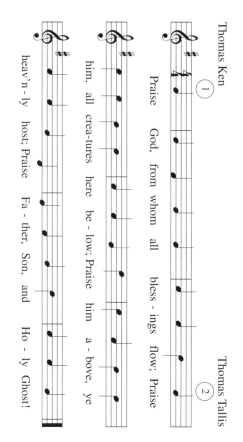

Praise God, from whom all bless - ings flow; Praise

him, all crea - tures here be - low; Praise him a - bove, ye

heav'n - ly host; Praise Fa - ther, Son, and Ho - ly Ghost!

THE MESSAGE Our Refuge

God is our refuge and strength, an ever-present help in trouble. Therefore we will not fear, though the earth give way and the mountains fall into the heart of the sea, though its waters roar and foam and the mountains quake with their surging (Psalm 46:1-3).

Leader: Dear God, you are our greatest refuge and strength. When troubles come, remind us that we do not need to be afraid. Teach us to come boldly to you in prayer. Help us trust that you will use your power to protect us. We ask this in Jesus' name. Amen.

HYMN A Mighty Fortress Is Our God

A mighty fortress is our God,
A trusty shield and weapon;
He helps us free from ev'ry need
That has us now o'ertaken.
The old evil foe Now means deadly woe;
Deep guile and great might Are his dread arms in fight;
On earth is not his equal.

With might of ours can naught be done;
Soon were our loss effected.
But for us fights the valiant one
Whom God himself elected.
You ask, "Who is this?" Jesus Christ it is,
The almighty Lord. And there's no other God;
He holds the field forever.

PSALM 46

Leader: God is our refuge and strength,

Children: **An ever-present help in trouble.**

Leader: Therefore we will not fear, though the earth give way

Children: **And the mountains fall into the heart of the sea,**

Leader: The LORD Almighty is with us;

Children: **The God of Jacob is our fortress.**

PRAYER REQUESTS

THE LORD'S PRAYER (*spoken together*)

OFFERINGS OF LOVE FOR JESUS

Leader: Now, children, go in peace. Live in harmony with one another. Serve the Lord with gladness. The grace of our Lord ☩ Jesus Christ and the love of God and the fellowship of the Holy Spirit be with you all.

Children: **Amen.**

Safe in Our Fortress
Psalm 46:4-7

Suggested for November 3–7, 2003

Visual Materials

- a toy castle or a picture of a castle

Object Lesson

Show the castle and ask: What is this? Why were castles built long ago? Explain that a castle is a type of fortress. A fortress is built to be a place of refuge for everyone inside—a place where people can find safety from their enemies. Such a fortress would be built with high, thick walls and a heavy door that would be shut and secured if an enemy came near. Point out that the group will hear God compared to a fortress in today's psalm.

Bible Truth

Psalm 46:4-7 says: **"There is a river whose streams make glad the city of God, the holy place where the Most High dwells. God is within her, she will not fall; God will help her at break of day. Nations are in uproar, kingdoms fall; he lifts his voice, the earth melts. The LORD Almighty is with us; the God of Jacob is our fortress."**

Explain that "the city of God" is God's church—his believers here on earth and in heaven. In the book of Revelation, our eternal home is described as a well-protected city. Psalm 46 says that God is within his city, protecting it and taking care of his people.

Our God, who has the power to simply speak the word and cause the earth to melt, is with his believers both in heaven and on earth. He is our fortress, providing safety when enemies such as the devil, temptations, and troubles are near. In such times God will help us stay faithful to him as he takes care of our needs. How comforting it is to know that God, our fortress, is always with us!

Discussions and Applications

1. Give examples of times when we need to remember that God is our fortress.

2. How does God bring people into his fortress?

CHAPEL TALKS FOR CHRISTIAN CHILDREN

NOVEMBER 3–7, 2003

Leader: As children of God, we worship the Lord our Savior.

Children: Let us unite our hearts and voices to praise his holy name.

SONG OF PRAISE Praise God, from Whom All Blessings Flow

Thomas Ken

Thomas Tallis

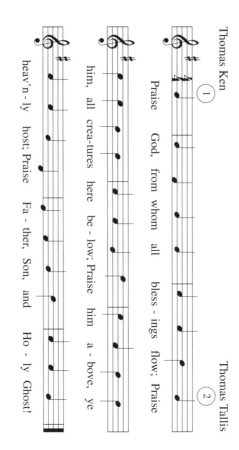

Praise God, from whom all bless - ings flow; Praise

him, all crea-tures here be - low; Praise him a - bove, ye

heav'n - ly host; Praise Fa - ther, Son, and Ho - ly Ghost!

THE MESSAGE Safe in Our Fortress

There is a river whose streams make glad the city of God, the holy place where the Most High dwells. God is within her, she will not fall; God will help her at break of day. Nations are in uproar, kingdoms fall; he lifts his voice, the earth melts. The LORD Almighty is with us; the God of Jacob is our fortress (Psalm 46:4-7).

Leader: Almighty Lord, we often face times of trouble in this world and need to hurry to you, our fortress, for safety. What a blessing it is to know that you are with us at all times! Help us trust that you will always be with us in every situation, protecting us with your mighty power. Amen.

HYMN A Mighty Fortress Is Our God

Though devils all the world should fill,
All eager to devour us,
We tremble not, we fear no ill;
They shall not overpow'r us.
This world's prince may still Scowl fierce as he will,
He can harm us none. He's judged; the deed is done!
One little word can fell him.

**The Word they still shall let remain,
Nor any thanks have for it;
He's by our side upon the plain
With his good gifts and Spirit.
And do what they will—Hate, steal, hurt, or kill—
Though all may be gone, Our victory is won;
The kingdom's ours forever!**

PSALM 46

Leader: God is our refuge and strength,

Children: An ever-present help in trouble.

Leader: There is a river whose streams make glad the city of God,

Children: The holy place where the Most High dwells.

Leader: God is within her, she will not fall;

Children: God will help her at break of day.

Leader: The LORD Almighty is with us;

Children: The God of Jacob is our fortress.

PRAYER REQUESTS

THE LORD'S PRAYER *(spoken together)*

OFFERINGS OF LOVE FOR JESUS

Leader: Now, children, go in peace. Live in harmony with one another. Serve the Lord with gladness.
The grace of our Lord + Jesus Christ and the love of God and the fellowship of the Holy Spirit be with you all.

Children: Amen.

Be Still
Psalm 46:8-11

Suggested for November 10–14, 2003

Visual Materials

- pictures of various weapons from both Bible times (such as a bow and arrow, a shield, or a spear) and modern times (such as a gun or fighter plane), if possible

Object Lesson

Show the pictures of weapons. Discuss how the weapons armies use may have changed since Bible times, but all are frightening to enemies. Remind the children that no matter how powerful any weapon may be, God's power is far greater.

Bible Truth

The final portion of **Psalm 46, verses 8-11,** says: **"Come and see the works of the Lord, the desolations he has brought on the earth. He makes wars cease to the ends of the earth; he breaks the bow and shatters the spear, he burns the shields with fire. 'Be still, and know that I am God; I will be exalted among the nations, I will be exalted in the earth.' The Lord Almighty is with us; the God of Jacob is our fortress."**

Ask: Can you think of times when God brought destruction to a powerful city or army? When we hear of accounts like the destruction of Sodom and Gomorrah, the drowning of Pharaoh's army in the Red Sea, and the fall of Jericho, we are reminded that God has sometimes, for the good of his people, brought desolation on the earth. But he also has the power to make wars stop and to break, shatter, and burn powerful weapons used by the wicked.

Explain that knowing how powerful God is can be frightening to his enemies. But to us, his people, God says, "Be still." God doesn't want us to live in fear, afraid of what evil people in this world will do. Instead, he tells us to remember that he is God. He protects us now. And on judgment day, he will end all wars forever. On that day people of all nations will see him and know that he is truly the almighty God.

Discussions and Applications

1. How can this psalm be especially comforting to us when we hear frightening things about war and terrorists on the news?

2. How is God's Word a weapon for his people?

CHAPEL TALKS FOR CHRISTIAN CHILDREN
NOVEMBER 10–14, 2003

Leader: As children of God, we worship the Lord our Savior.

Children: Let us unite our hearts and voices to praise his holy name.

SONG OF PRAISE Praise God, from Whom All Blessings Flow

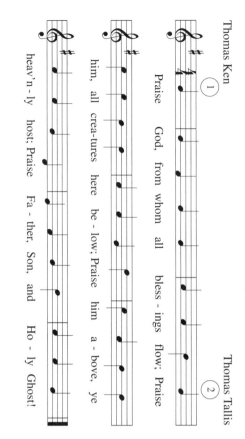

Thomas Ken

Thomas Tallis

① Praise God, from whom all bless - ings flow; Praise

him, all crea - tures here be - low; Praise him a - bove, ye

heav'n - ly host; Praise Fa - ther, Son, and Ho - ly Ghost!

THE MESSAGE Be Still

Come and see the works of the LORD, the desolations he has brought on the earth. He makes wars cease to the ends of the earth; he breaks the bow and shatters the spear; he burns the shields with fire. "Be still, and know that I am God; I will be exalted among the nations, I will be exalted in the earth." The LORD Almighty is with us; the God of Jacob is our fortress (Psalm 46:8-11).

Leader: Heavenly Father, this world can be a frightening place. We often hear of evil people who want to use powerful weapons against us. When we begin to feel afraid, remind us that you are more powerful than any person, weapon, or army. Teach us to "be still," knowing that

you are our God, who protects us. We ask this in the name of Jesus, who has already defeated our most powerful enemy, the devil. Amen.

HYMN Be Still, My Soul

Be still, my soul; the Lord is on your side;
Bear patiently the cross of grief or pain;
Leave to your God to order and provide;
In ev'ry change he faithful will remain.
Be still, my soul; your best, your heav'nly friend
Through thorny ways leads to a joyful end.

Be still, my soul; your God will undertake
To guide the future as he has the past.
Your hope, your confidence, let nothing shake;
All now mysterious shall be bright at last.
Be still, my soul; the waves and winds still know
His voice who ruled them while he lived below.

PSALM 46

Leader: The LORD Almighty is with us;

Children: The God of Jacob is our fortress.

Leader: "Be still, and know that I am God;

Children: I will be exalted among the nations, I will be exalted in the earth."

Leader: The LORD Almighty is with us;

Children: The God of Jacob is our fortress.

PRAYER REQUESTS

THE LORD'S PRAYER (*spoken together*)

OFFERINGS OF LOVE FOR JESUS

Leader: Now, children, go in peace. Live in harmony with one another. Serve the LORD with gladness. The grace of our Lord ✠ Jesus Christ and the love of God and the fellowship of the Holy Spirit be with you all.

Children: Amen.

Dream House
Psalm 84:1,2

Suggested for November 17–21, 2003

Visual Materials

- different pictures of houses

Object Lesson

Ask the children: What is your dream house? If you could design your own home, what would it look like? (These are rhetorical questions.) Show them the different pictures of houses. You might show a duplex, a ranch-style home, a two-story house, a hut, a mansion, and so on. Ask them which ones they would pick.

Show a picture of your house. Explain that this may not be their dream home, but it is home. Talk about times after a long trip when you looked forward to getting home and sleeping in your own bed.

Bible Truth

Psalm 84:1,2 says: **"How lovely is your dwelling place, O Lord Almighty! My soul yearns, even faints, for the courts of the Lord; my heart and my flesh cry out for the living God."**

Thinking and talking about your dream home can be fun. Maybe someday you'll have your dream home on earth. Can you imagine what Adam and Eve must have felt living in paradise? They are the only humans who ever existed in perfection with God. They are also the only humans who ever experienced the difference between living in paradise and living in sin. They knew both experiences well.

Our destination was like that of Adam and Eve. We were doomed to another place that we wouldn't have dreamed of (hell) because of our sins. We know what earth is like now. There is violence, crime, and rebellion. People despise and hate one another. Sometimes our houses are not the most wonderful places to live either.

We, like the psalmist, long for a new home. God sent his Son to take away our sins by dying on the cross and gave us a new home and destination, heaven. While we often wonder what our heavenly dream house will be like, God gives us a taste by describing it as a mansion, a place with streets of gold, where there will be no more tears. God's love and grace make it possible for all believers to live in their dream houses someday in heaven.

Discussions and Applications

1. How would you describe heaven to someone who doesn't know about it?

2. What things in our earthly homes weaken our desires for our heavenly home?

CHAPEL TALKS FOR CHRISTIAN CHILDREN
NOVEMBER 17–21, 2003

Leader: As children of God, we worship the Lord our Savior.

Children: **Let us unite our hearts and voices to praise his holy name.**

SONG OF PRAISE Praise God, from Whom All Blessings Flow

Thomas Ken

Thomas Tallis

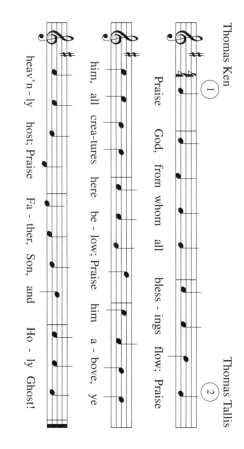

Praise God, from whom all bless-ings flow; Praise him, all crea-tures here be-low; Praise him a-bove, ye heav'n-ly host; Praise Fa-ther, Son, and Ho-ly Ghost!

HYMN I'm But a Stranger Here

I'm but a stranger here; Heav'n is my home.
Earth is a desert drear; Heav'n is my home.
Danger and sorrow stand Round me on ev'ry hand.
Heav'n is my fatherland; Heav'n is my home.

There at my Savior's side —Heav'n is my home—
I shall be glorified; Heav'n is my home.
There are the good and blest, Those I love most
and best,
And there, I, too, shall rest; Heav'n is my home.

PSALM 84

Leader: How lovely is your dwelling place,

Children: **O Lord Almighty!**

Leader: My soul yearns, even faints,

Children: **For the courts of the LORD;**

Leader: My heart and my flesh

Children: **Cry out for the living God.**

Leader: Blessed are those who dwell in your house;

Children: **They are ever praising you.**

PRAYER REQUESTS

THE LORD'S PRAYER *(spoken together)*

OFFERINGS OF LOVE FOR JESUS

Leader: Now, children, go in peace. Live in harmony with one another. Serve the Lord with gladness.

The grace of our Lord ☩ Jesus Christ and the love of God and the fellowship of the Holy Spirit be with you all.

Children: **Amen.**

THE MESSAGE Dream House

How lovely is your dwelling place, O LORD Almighty! My soul yearns, even faints, for the courts of the LORD; my heart and my flesh cry out for the living God (Psalm 84:1,2).

Leader: Loving Lord, how wonderful it is to think of eternal pleasures at your right hand. Help us focus on our heavenly home at all times until you take us to be with you forever. Amen.

Stay in the Nest
Psalm 84:3,4

Suggested for November 24–28, 2003

Visual Materials

- pictures of animal habitats

- a bird's nest

Object Lesson

Show the pictures of habitats (homes) of different animals. Suggestions might include: an aquarium (fish), a cave (bears, bats), an anthill (ants), and so on. Have students tell who lives in what dwelling. For the final home, show a bird's nest.

Bible Truth

Psalm 84:3,4 reads: **"Even the sparrow has found a home, and the swallow a nest for herself, where she may have her young—a place near your altar, O LORD Almighty, my King and my God. Blessed are those who dwell in your house; they are ever praising you."**

Ask: How many of you would like to live in a bird's nest? Would it be a little crowded? Would you even fit? Would it be a little dirty? Would it offer you enough protection from the weather?

Where does God dwell? Where is his nest? You might say heaven, and you would be right. However, he is also right here right now. In fact we call this God's house, a place where God dwells.

It might seem a little strange that the psalmist is talking about birds' nests and God's house. The connection is that he is a little envious. The birds have built nests close to God's altar, or God's temple. The psalmist longs to be that close to God as well.

Before we became believers, we did not have access to God's house. Our sin caused the door of God's house to be closed to us. Jesus has now opened that door for us through his perfect life, death, and resurrection. We are now free to worship and praise God in his house, the place where we are today. Just as a nest provides safety and comfort for birds, so God's house gives us strength and comfort. In this house we praise our good and gracious God for everything he does for us day in and day out.

Discussions and Applications

1. What causes us to "fall out of God's nest"?

2. How do we show respect in God's house?

CHAPEL TALKS FOR CHRISTIAN CHILDREN

NOVEMBER 24–28, 2003

Leader: As children of God, we worship the Lord our Savior.

Children: Let us unite our hearts and voices to praise his holy name.

SONG OF PRAISE Praise God, from Whom All Blessings Flow

Thomas Ken

Thomas Tallis

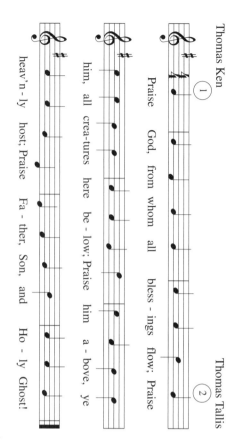

Praise God, from whom all bless - ings flow; Praise him, all crea-tures here be - low; Praise him a - bove, ye heav'n - ly host; Praise Fa - ther, Son, and Ho - ly Ghost!

THE MESSAGE Stay in the Nest

Even the sparrow has found a home, and the swallow a nest for herself, where she may have her young—a place near your altar, O LORD Almighty, my King and my God. Blessed are those who dwell in your house; they are ever praising you (Psalm 84:3,4).

Leader: Heavenly Father, thank you for teaching us about you. Give us hearts that are always eager to learn, putting you high in our minds and our lives. Let us worship you and stay close to you. Amen.

HYMN Children of the Heavenly Father*

Children of the heav'nly Father
Safely in his bosom gather;
Nestling bird or star in heaven
Such a refuge ne'er was given.

God his own doth tend and nourish;
In his holy courts they flourish.
From all evil things he spares them;
In his mighty arms he bears them.

Neither life nor death shall ever
From the Lord his children sever;
Unto them his grace he showeth,
And their sorrows all he knoweth.

Though he giveth or he taketh,
God his children ne'er forsaketh;
His the loving purpose solely
To preserve them pure and holy.

PSALM 84

Leader: Blessed are those who dwell in your house;

Children: They are ever praising you.

Leader: Better is one day in your courts

Children: Than a thousand elsewhere;

Leader: I would rather be a doorkeeper in the house of my God

Children: Than dwell in the tents of the wicked.

Leader: O LORD Almighty,

Children: Blessed is the man who trusts in you.

PRAYER REQUESTS

THE LORD'S PRAYER *(spoken together)*

OFFERINGS OF LOVE FOR JESUS

Leader: Now, children, go in peace. Live in harmony with one another. Serve the Lord with gladness.

The grace of our Lord ✠ Jesus Christ and the love of God and the fellowship of the Holy Spirit be with you all.

Children: Amen.

*Text: © Board of Publication, Lutheran Church in America. Reprinted by permission of Augsburg Fortress.

A Humble Servant
Luke 1:46-49

Suggested for December 1–5, 2003

Visual Materials

- a pair of dirty shoes or a dirty dish

Object Lesson

Bring out a pair of dirty shoes or a dirty dish, and ask a volunteer to clean it for you. Notice the reaction. Did the volunteer look discouraged or reluctant? Did he or she jump in and start cleaning?

Another option is to have an older student tie the shoe of a younger student. Discuss the older student's response. Is he or she reluctant? Note how each volunteer serves the other person.

Bible Truth

Luke 1:46-49 reads: **"Mary said: 'My soul glorifies the Lord and my spirit rejoices in God my Savior, for he has been mindful of the humble state of his servant. From now on all generations will call me blessed, for the Mighty One has done great things for me—holy is his name.'"**

Ask the children to think of all the mothers who have ever lived, are living now, or who will be mothers in the future. Yet God chose one, Mary, the mother of Jesus, to be the mother of the Savior of the world.

Mary was a sinner just like you and me. In fact she refers to God as her Savior in her beautiful song. Yet God took this sinner and, through a wonderful miracle, used her to be the one to bring Jesus into this world.

How many mothers wouldn't feel privileged to be the one to bring the Savior into the world? In fact, some might even brag or be proud of this. Not Mary. She is a tremendous example of humility. She understood that she was a humble servant in God's plan. She gave all the glory and honor to God, who not only blessed her with the gift of a Savior but has blessed everyone in the whole world. Her song glorifies God for the wonderful things he has done.

Discussions and Applications

1. How have you served God this week?

2. Why is serving with humility so important?

CHAPEL TALKS FOR CHRISTIAN CHILDREN
DECEMBER 1–5, 2003

Leader: As children of God, we worship the Lord our Savior.

Children: **Let us unite our hearts and voices to praise his holy name.**

SONG OF PRAISE Joy to the World

Isaac Watts

George F. Handel

Leader: Dear Lord, thank you for your amazing love for us. Help us always remember how wonderful your works are on our behalf. Make us humble servants in your kingdom. Amen.

HYMN Savior of the Nations, Come

Savior of the nations, come;
Virgin's Son, make here your home.
Marvel now, O heav'n and earth,
That the Lord chose such a birth.

Not by human flesh and blood,
By the Spirit of our God
Was the Word of God made flesh,
Woman's offspring, pure and fresh.

Wondrous birth! O wondrous Child
Of the virgin undefiled,
Though by all the world disowned,
Yet to be in heav'n enthroned!

PSALM 35

Leader: My soul will rejoice in the LORD

Children: **And delight in his salvation.**

Leader: My whole being will exclaim,

Children: **"Who is like you, O LORD?**

Leader: You rescue the poor from those too strong for them,

Children: **The poor and needy from those who rob them."**

PRAYER REQUESTS

THE LORD'S PRAYER (*spoken together*)

OFFERINGS OF LOVE FOR JESUS

Leader: Now, children, go in peace. Live in harmony with one another. Serve the Lord with gladness.

The grace of our Lord ✝ Jesus Christ and the love of God and the fellowship of the Holy Spirit be with you all.

Children: **Amen.**

THE MESSAGE A Humble Servant

Mary said: "My soul glorifies the Lord and my spirit rejoices in God my Savior, for he has been mindful of the humble state of his servant. From now on all generations will call me blessed, for the Mighty One has done great things for me—holy is his name" (*Luke 1:46-49*).

The Arm of God
Luke 1:50-52

Suggested for December 8–12, 2003

Visual Materials

- a Frisbee, football, or baseball
- a picture of weightlifter's or bodybuilder's arm

Object Lesson

Solicit from the group ideas of how you use your arms in everyday life. Demonstrate these uses to the children. You might throw a Frisbee or do a push-up.

Show the picture of a weightlifter or bodybuilder. Note the strength of his arms. Point out that the Song of Mary continues to tell about God's strength.

Bible Truth

Luke 1:50-52 says: **"His mercy extends to those who fear him, from generation to generation. He has performed mighty deeds with his arm; he has scattered those who are proud in their inmost thoughts. He has brought down rulers from their thrones but has lifted up the humble."**

In the Bible, God is given human characteristics at times. Although God does not have a body, they help us picture God in a different way. God's arm is often used in the Bible to show his strength and power.

What has God done with his mighty arm in history? (Solicit answers from the crowd, or share the following examples.) God once destroyed the cities of Sodom and Gomorrah. God destroyed all of Pharaoh's army during the days of the plagues. God crumbled the walls of Jericho and led the nation of Israel to many victories on its path to the Promised Land.

Does God's arm frighten you? At times it may. When we hear of God scattering the proud in our text, we look at ourselves. There are times when our sin causes us to be proud. The warning is there for us: if we do not change our ways and ask for forgiveness, God will bring us down.

Does God's arm bring comfort? Yes, it does. He lifts up the humble in spirit and protects his people from harm. This is comforting because we have a God who is the strongest in the whole universe, and he has us in his hand, protecting us from all harm.

Discussions and Applications

1. How has God displayed his "mighty arm" in your life?

2. What causes us to become sinfully proud?

CHAPEL TALKS FOR CHRISTIAN CHILDREN
DECEMBER 8–12, 2003

Leader: As children of God, we worship the Lord our Savior.

Children: Let us unite our hearts and voices to praise his holy name.

SONG OF PRAISE *Joy to the World*

Isaac Watts   George F. Handel

1. Joy	to the world, the Lord is come! Let
2. Joy	to the earth, the Sav - ior reigns! Let

earth re - ceive her King; While fields and

all their songs em - ploy, Let ev - 'ry

heart and floods, rocks, hills, and plains pre - pare him room And heav'n and Re - peat the

na - ture sing, And heav'n and na - ture sing, And

sound - ing joy, Re - peat the sound - ing joy,

heav'n,— and heav'n and na - ture sing.

re - peat, re - peat the sound - ing joy.

Leader: Lord, you are our protector. You are our strength and salvation. Keep us in the faith always, that we may join you one day in the unending safety of heaven. Amen.

HYMN *Hark the Glad Sound! The Savior Comes*

Hark the glad sound! The Savior comes,
The Savior promised long;
Let ev'ry heart prepare a throne
And ev'ry voice a song;

He comes the captives to release,
In Satan's prison held.
The gates of brass before him burst;
The iron fetters yield.

He comes the broken heart to bind,
The bleeding soul to cure,
And with the treasures of his grace
To enrich the humble poor.

PSALM 2

Leader: Why do the nations conspire

Children: And the peoples plot in vain?

Leader: The One enthroned in heaven laughs;

Children: The Lord scoffs at them.

Leader: Then he rebukes them in his anger

Children: And terrifies them in his wrath, saying,

All: "I have installed my King on Zion, my holy hill."

PRAYER REQUESTS

THE LORD'S PRAYER (*spoken together*)

OFFERINGS OF LOVE FOR JESUS

Leader: Now, children, go in peace. Live in harmony with one another. Serve the Lord with gladness. The grace of our Lord ✛ Jesus Christ and the love of God and the fellowship of the Holy Spirit be with you all.

Children: Amen.

THE MESSAGE The Arm of God

"*His mercy extends to those who fear him, from generation to generation. He has performed mighty deeds with his arm; he has scattered those who are proud in their inmost thoughts. He has brought down rulers from their thrones but has lifted up the humble*" (*Luke 1:50-52*).

Food for Thought
Luke 1:53-55

Suggested for December 15–19, 2003

Visual Materials

- physical foods (snacks, fruits, drinks, etc.)
- spiritual foods (Bible, hymnal, catechism, prayer book, music)

Object Lesson

Ask the children what they eat when they are really hungry. Solicit a few responses. Show the kids what you like to eat when you are really hungry by pulling some of the food from a bag.

Bible Truth

God wants us to eat and drink to nourish our bodies. We need food to stay strong and be productive in all our activities. However, our text today talks about another kind of hunger. It is recorded in the Song of Mary in **Luke 1:53-55: "He has filled the hungry with good things but has sent the rich away empty. He has helped his servant Israel, remembering to be merciful to Abraham and his descendants forever, even as he said to our fathers."**

God is more concerned about our spiritual hunger. This is the most dangerous kind of hunger, because it can hurt our souls. Just as we sometimes eat things that aren't good for us or upset our stomachs, our spiritual lives are affected by sin. Depression, frustration, rebellion, and loneliness can make us spiritually hungry.

God wants us to take care of our spiritual hunger. What are your favorite spiritual foods that help comfort or remind you of God's promises and God's forgiveness? (Solicit responses and then show the children what you have in your bag of "spiritual food.") All these things remind us that we are sinners in need of God's forgiveness and that in his mercy Jesus is our Savior from that sin.

Discussions and Applications

1. How do you know when you are spiritually hungry?

2. What can you do for others who are spiritually hungry?

CHAPEL TALKS FOR CHRISTIAN CHILDREN
DECEMBER 15–19, 2003

Leader: As children of God, we worship the Lord our Savior.
Children: Let us unite our hearts and voices to praise his holy name.

SONG OF PRAISE *Joy to the World*

Isaac Watts

George F. Handel

1. Joy to the world, the Lord is come! Let
2. Joy to the earth, the Sav - ior reigns! Let

earth re - ceive her King; Let ev - 'ry
all their songs em - ploy, While fields_ and_

heart pre - pare him_ room, And heav'n and
floods,_ rocks, hills,_ and_ plains Re - peat the

na - ture sing, And heav'n and na - ture_ sing, And_
sound - ing joy, Re - peat the sound - ing_ joy,_ Re -

heav'n,_ and heav'n_ and na - ture sing.
peat,_ re - peat_ the sound - ing joy.

THE MESSAGE Food for Thought

"He has filled the hungry with good things but has sent the rich away empty. He has helped his servant Israel, remembering to be merciful to Abraham and his descendants forever, even as he said to our fathers" (Luke 1:53-55).

Leader: Praise the Lord, O my soul, and forget not all his blessings. He crowns us with love and compassion. He satisfies our desires with good things. Amen.

HYMN Let the Earth Now Praise the Lord

Let the earth now praise the Lord,
Who has truly kept his word
And at last to us did send
Christ, the sinner's help and friend.

What the fathers most desired,
What the prophets' heart inspired,
What they longed for many a year
Stands fulfilled in glory here.

Abram's promised great reward,
Zion's helper, Jacob's Lord—
Him of twofold race behold—
Truly came, as long foretold.

Welcome, O my Savior, now!
Joyful, Lord, to you I bow.
Come into my heart, I pray;
Oh, prepare yourself a way.

PSALM 107

Leader: Give thanks to the LORD, for he is good;
Children: His love endures forever.
Leader: Let the redeemed of the LORD say this—
Children: Those he redeemed from the hand of the foe,
Leader: Let them give thanks to the LORD for his unfailing love
Children: And his wonderful deeds for men,
Leader: For he satisfies the thirsty
Children: And fills the hungry with good things.

PRAYER REQUESTS

THE LORD'S PRAYER (*spoken together*)

OFFERINGS OF LOVE FOR JESUS

Leader: Now, children, go in peace. Live in harmony with one another. Serve the Lord with gladness.

The grace of our Lord ✝ Jesus Christ and the love of God and the fellowship of the Holy Spirit be with you all.

Children: Amen.

A Special Invitation
Luke 2:14

Suggested for December 22–26, 2003

Visual Materials

- a selection of different invitations or announcements for birthday parties, anniversaries, baptisms, weddings, or announcements of sales from stores

Object Lesson

Ask the children what they have received invitations to. Ask them why people send out invitations or announcements.

Show children different examples of invitations or announcements you have received, and discuss them briefly. You might also share some appealing announcements from stores and restaurants in your local area.

Bible Truth

Angels announce in **Luke 2:14, "Glory to God in the highest, and on earth peace to men on whom his favor rests."**

The time had come for God to announce that the Savior of the world was to be born in Bethlehem. Ask: How did God do it? Did he have a person announce the news with a trumpet? Did God send out invitations or have it proclaimed in the temple courts or marketplaces of different towns? Did God write it up in the sky in big letters?

God chose to use his angels to proclaim the news in song. The song is one you know very well. In Latin it is called *Gloria in Excelsis,* or "Glory to God in the Highest." God used a heavenly choir with glorious voices to announce the birth of his Son, the Savior of the world. Can you think of a better way than that?

Wouldn't it have been wonderful to be in that audience? The shepherds received a special invitation from God to come see the Savior and heard a beautiful concert all at the same time.

The invitation comes to us every Christmas. We are reminded of our sins and need for a Savior. We are overjoyed to once again hear the angels singing and sharing that special invitation to come to Bethlehem and find the only lasting peace for our souls in Jesus, our Savior from sin.

Discussions and Applications

1. How can we announce the birth of Christ to our community?

2. How can Christmas parties and decorations distract us from God's wonderful announcement to the world?

CHAPEL TALKS FOR CHRISTIAN CHILDREN
DECEMBER 22-26, 2003

Leader: As children of God, we worship the Lord our Savior.

Children: **Let us unite our hearts and voices to praise his holy name.**

SONG OF PRAISE *Joy to the World*

Isaac Watts

George F. Handel

1. Joy to the world, the Lord is come! Let earth receive her King; Let ev'ry heart prepare him room While fields, and floods, rocks, hills, and plains Repeat the sounding joy.

2. Joy to the earth, the Savior reigns! Let all their songs employ; While fields and floods, rocks, hills, and plains Repeat the sounding joy, Repeat, Repeat the sounding joy. And heav'n and nature sing, And heav'n and nature sing, And heav'n, and heav'n and nature sing.

THE MESSAGE A Special Invitation

"Glory to God in the highest, and on earth peace to men on whom his favor rests" (Luke 2:14).

Leader: O dear Father, send your powerful Word to those who need a change in their hearts. Show us how to share this powerful message of salvation. Bless our words and actions through your dear Son, our Savior. Amen.

HYMN Hark! The Herald Angels Sing

Hark! The herald angels sing,
"Glory to the newborn King;
Peace on earth and mercy mild,
God and sinners reconciled!"
Joyful, all you nations rise,
Join the triumph of the skies;
With th' angelic host proclaim,
"Christ is born in Bethlehem!"
Hark! The herald angels sing,
"Glory to the newborn King!"

Christ, by highest heav'n adored,
Christ, the everlasting Lord,
Late in time behold him come,
Offspring of a virgin's womb.
Veiled in flesh the Godhead see,
Hail th' incarnate Deity!
Pleased as man with us to dwell,
Jesus, our Immanuel!
Hark! The herald angels sing,
"Glory to the newborn King!"

PSALM 103

Leader: Praise the LORD, you his angels,

Children: **You mighty ones who do his bidding, who obey his word.**

Leader: Praise the LORD, all his heavenly hosts,

Children: **You his servants who do his will.**

Leader: Praise the LORD, all his works everywhere in his dominion.

Children: **Praise the LORD, O my soul.**

PRAYER REQUESTS

THE LORD'S PRAYER *(spoken together)*

OFFERINGS OF LOVE FOR JESUS

Leader: Now, children, go in peace. Live in harmony with one another. Serve the Lord with gladness.

The grace of our Lord ✠ Jesus Christ and the love of God and the fellowship of the Holy Spirit be with you all.

Children: **Amen.**

A Sight for Sore Eyes
Luke 2:29-32

Suggested for December 29, 2003–January 2, 2004

Visual Materials

- pictures of favorite places you want to visit or people you would like to meet

Object Lesson

Ask: What are some places you would like to see before you die? Why do you want to see these places? Are there people you would like to meet? Show the children pictures of places you would like to visit.

Bible Truth

Luke 2:29-32 says: **"Sovereign Lord, as you have promised, you now dismiss your servant in peace. For my eyes have seen your salvation, which you have prepared in the sight of all people, a light for revelation to the Gentiles and for glory to your people Israel."**

These words were spoken by Simeon, a man described as righteous and devout. The words have been put to music as the Song of Simeon in our hymnal. God had promised Simeon that he would not die until he had seen the Savior with his own eyes.

God kept his promise. When Mary and Joseph brought Jesus to the temple, Simeon took him in his arms and praised God with the words of his song. Simeon had longed to see the Savior before he died. After seeing and holding him, he could die in peace, knowing that he had seen his Savior from sin, just as God had promised.

We also long to see our Savior. Like Simeon, we are sinful. True peace could not be given to us because of our sin, and we were doomed to a place where there is weeping and gnashing of teeth—hell. However, we see our Savior with the eyes of faith. Although it may be different than what Simeon experienced—we haven't held Jesus with our own arms—the effect is still the same. The Savior that came for Simeon also came for us. He is our Savior from sin. Our eyes of faith hold Jesus close to our hearts. We look forward to the day when we will see Jesus in heaven with our own eyes.

Discussions and Applications

1. How do we lead the blind (lost souls) to see Jesus?

2. How does seeing Jesus help us in our daily living?

CHAPEL TALKS FOR CHRISTIAN CHILDREN
DECEMBER 29, 2003–JANUARY 2, 2004

Leader: As children of God, we worship the Lord our Savior.

Children: **Let us unite our hearts and voices to praise his holy name.**

SONG OF PRAISE Joy to the World

Isaac Watts

George F. Handel

Leader: Dear Jesus, thank you for coming to earth to take away our sins. Help us share the spiritual wealth of joy, peace, and the hope of heaven with many other people. Amen.

HYMN In Peace and Joy I Now Depart

In peace and joy I now depart As my Lord wills it;
Serene and quiet is my heart; Gladness fills it.
This the Lord has promised me, That death is but
a slumber.

Christ Jesus brought this gift to me, My faithful Savior,
Whom you allowed my eyes to see By your favor.
Now I know he is my life, My friend when I am dying.

PSALM 98

Leader: The LORD has made his salvation known

Children: **And revealed his righteousness to the nations.**

Leader: He has remembered his love and his faithfulness to the house of Israel;

Children: **All the ends of the earth have seen the salvation of our God.**

Leader: Shout for joy to the LORD, all the earth,

Children: **Burst into jubilant song with music.**

PRAYER REQUESTS

THE LORD'S PRAYER *(spoken together)*

OFFERINGS OF LOVE FOR JESUS

Leader: Now, children, go in peace. Live in harmony with one another. Serve the Lord with gladness.

The grace of our Lord ☩ Jesus Christ and the love of God and the fellowship of the Holy Spirit be with you all.

Children: Amen.

THE MESSAGE A Sight for Sore Eyes

"Sovereign Lord, as you have promised, you now dismiss your servant in peace. For my eyes have seen your salvation, which you have prepared in the sight of all people, a light for revelation to the Gentiles and for glory to your people Israel" (Luke 2:29-32).

Horn of Strength
Luke 1:67-75

Suggested for January 5–9, 2004

Visual Materials

- an animal horn, if you can find one
- pictures of animals with horns

Object Lesson

Ask the children for examples of animals with horns. Show pictures of the animals you anticipate they might say. Ask: Why do animals have horns? What would happen if they didn't have horns?

Mention that John the Baptist's father, Zechariah, talks about a horn of salvation in his song, and encourage the children to listen to what he says.

Bible Truth

Luke 1:67-75 says: **"His father Zechariah was filled with the Holy Spirit and prophesied: 'Praise be to the Lord, the God of Israel, because he has come and has redeemed his people. He has raised up a horn of salvation for us in the house of his servant David (as he said through his holy prophets of long ago), salvation from our enemies and from the hand of all who hate us—to show mercy to our fathers and to remember his holy covenant, the oath he swore to our father Abraham: to rescue us from the hand of our enemies, and to enable us to serve him without fear in holiness and righteousness before him all our days.' "**

We have a lot of enemies. The three we speak of often are the devil, the world, and our sinful flesh. The devil attacks us day after day. The world tries to deceive us and lead us into sin with its different traps. Our sinful flesh is an enemy of God and doesn't want to follow the ways of God. These enemies lead us to destruction and eternal hellfire.

How do we escape? In order to overcome these enemies, we need someone strong to protect us, someone with great power to deliver us from the depths of hell and bring us to eternal life. Jesus is our deliverer. Zechariah calls him the "horn of salvation." Just as an animal uses a horn to defeat its enemies, Jesus—our horn—defeated sin, death, and the devil. He is the one who brings salvation to us and protects us from those who would take it away. Just as an animal is very weak without its horns, so we as Christians are weak and defenseless without Jesus in our lives. He is the strength of our salvation. Only he can bring us true peace and comfort that enables us to serve him without fear all the days of our lives.

Discussions and Applications

1. What are some other pictures used to show that Jesus is strong?

2. Why do we want to take on our enemies by ourselves at times?

CHAPEL TALKS FOR CHRISTIAN CHILDREN

JANUARY 5–9, 2004

Leader: As children of God, we worship the Lord our Savior.

Children: **Let us unite our hearts and voices to praise his holy name.**

SONG OF PRAISE *Joy to the World*

Isaac Watts

George F. Handel

1. Joy to the world, the Lord is come! Let earth receive her King; Let ev'ry heart prepare him room And heav'n and na - ture sing, And heav'n and na - ture sing, And heav'n, and heav'n and na - ture sing.

2. Joy to the earth, the Sav - ior reigns! Let all their songs em - ploy; While fields and floods, rocks, hills, and plains Re - peat the sound-ing joy, Re - peat the sound-ing joy, Re - peat, re - peat the sound-ing joy.

THE MESSAGE Horn of Strength

His father Zechariah was filled with the Holy Spirit and prophesied: "Praise be to the Lord, the God of Israel, because he has come and redeemed his people. He has raised up a horn of salvation for us in the house of his servant David (as he said through his holy prophets of long ago), salvation from our enemies and from the hand of all who hate us—to show mercy to our fathers and to remember his holy covenant, the oath he

swore to our father Abraham: to rescue us from the hand of our enemies, and to enable us to serve him without fear in holiness and righteousness before him all our days" (Luke 1:67-75).

Leader: Dear Jesus, thank you for defeating sin, death, and the devil for us. Give us confidence in you as you reign as Savior of the world. Amen.

HYMN Jesus! Name of Wondrous Love

Jesus! Name of wondrous love,
Name all other names above,
Unto which must ev'ry knee
Bow in deep humility.

Jesus! Name decreed of old,
To the maiden mother told—
Kneeling in her lowly cell—
By the angel Gabriel.

Jesus! Name of priceless worth
To the fallen here on earth
For the promise that it gave,
"Jesus shall his people save."

PSALM 148

Leader: Let them praise the name of the LORD,

Children: **For his name alone is exalted;**

Leader: His splendor is above the earth

Children: **And the heavens.**

Leader: He has raised up for his people a horn,

Children: **The praise of all his saints, of Israel,**

Leader: The people close to his heart.

Children: **Praise the LORD.**

PRAYER REQUESTS

THE LORD'S PRAYER *(spoken together)*

OFFERINGS OF LOVE FOR JESUS

Leader: Now, children, go in peace. Live in harmony with one another. Serve the Lord with gladness.

The grace of our Lord ✝ Jesus Christ and the love of God and the fellowship of the Holy Spirit be with you all.

Children: **Amen.**

The Light
Luke 1:76-79

Suggested for January 12–16, 2004

Visual Materials

- a flashlight or lantern

Object Lesson

Describe a time when you were lost in the dark. Maybe it was during a storm when it was pitch dark inside. Maybe it was outside in a camping situation. Ask for volunteers to describe times when they were lost in the dark.

Turn out the lights as you describe that experience. Ask students what you can use to help you. Turn on your flashlight, and show how it leads you to safety.

Bible Truth

Luke 1:76-79 says, **"You, my child, will be called a prophet of the Most High; for you will go on before the Lord to prepare the way for him, to give his people the knowledge of salvation through the forgiveness of their sins, because of the tender mercy of our God, by which the rising sun will come to us from heaven to shine on those living in darkness and in the shadow of death, to guide our feet into the path of peace."**

When we are in complete darkness, we are paralyzed and lost. We crash into walls and stumble over furniture as we search for the ways to our destinations.

Complete darkness may be the best way to describe our relationship with God because of our sin. We stumble around looking for God but can't find him. Our sins create a canyon between God and us that we can't jump over or get across. We are lost and separated from God. We reach out but can't find him. We are truly lost and condemned creatures.

Zechariah's song reveals to us the light who leads us on the path of salvation. Jesus is the light who takes away the darkness. Jesus led the perfect life we could not lead. Jesus died and paid the price we could not pay. Jesus rose from the grave victorious over sin, death, and the devil. Now his light shows us the path to heaven. In a world that can lead us down different paths, Jesus' light dispels all darkness and shines brightly to keep us on the right path to eternal glory.

Discussions and Applications

1. What are other paths that mislead us?

2. How do you keep the light of Jesus burning bright in your life?

CHAPEL TALKS FOR CHRISTIAN CHILDREN
JANUARY 12-16, 2004

Leader: As children of God, we worship the Lord our Savior.

Children: Let us unite our hearts and voices to praise his holy name.

SONG OF PRAISE O God from God, O Light from Light

John Julian   *Johann Störls . . . Schlag-Gesang-Und Noten-Buch*

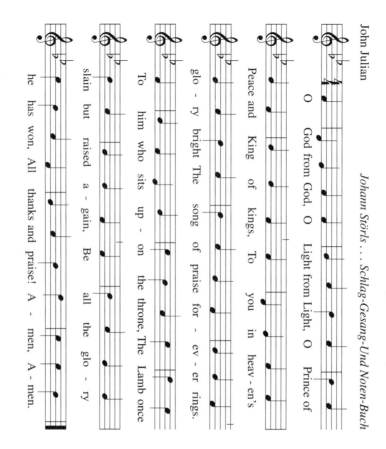

O God from God, O Light from Light, O Prince of

Peace and King of kings, To you in heav-en's

glo - ry bright The song of praise for - ev - er rings.

To him who sits up - on the throne, The Lamb once

slain but raised a - gain, Be all the glo - ry

he has won, All thanks and praise! A - men, A - men.

THE MESSAGE The Light

"You, my child, will be called a prophet of the Most High; for you will go on before the Lord to prepare the way for him, to give his people the knowledge of salvation through the forgiveness of their sins, because of the tender mercy of our God, by which the rising sun will come to us from heaven to shine on those living in darkness and in the shadow of death, to guide our feet into the path of peace" (Luke 1:76-79).

Leader: Dear Jesus, we praise and thank you for coming to be our holy substitute. Help us spread the good news about you as the Light of the world to those still living in darkness. Amen.

HYMN The People That in Darkness Sat

The people that in darkness sat
A glorious light have seen;
The light has shone on them who long
In shades of death have been, In shades of death
have been.

To us a child of hope is born,
To us a son is giv'n,
And on his shoulders ever rests
All pow'r in earth and heav'n, All pow'r in earth
and heav'n.

His name shall be the Prince of Peace,
The Everlasting Lord,
The Wonderful, the Counselor,
The God by all adored, The God by all adored.

PSALM 27

Leader: The LORD is my light and my salvation—

Children: Whom shall I fear?

Leader: The LORD is the stronghold of my life—

Children: Of whom shall I be afraid?

Leader: One thing I ask of the LORD, this is what I seek:

Children: That I may dwell in the house of the LORD all the days of my life.

PRAYER REQUESTS

THE LORD'S PRAYER (*spoken together*)

OFFERINGS OF LOVE FOR JESUS

Leader: Now, children, go in peace. Live in harmony with one another. Serve the Lord with gladness.

The grace of our Lord ✛ Jesus Christ and the love of God and the fellowship of the Holy Spirit be with you all.

Children: Amen.

No Fear
Isaiah 12:1,2

Suggested for January 19–23, 2004

Visual Materials

- a flashlight
- a teddy bear

Object Lesson

Show the flashlight and the teddy bear to the children. Ask: What do these two things have in common? When might we use both these items? What might they do for us? Explain that they may bring comfort to some children who are afraid of the dark. Flashlights can light up their bedrooms at home, and teddy bears to hug tight might make them feel better on dark, scary nights. Children might learn to make sure that their trustworthy flashlights or brave teddy bears are always close by at bedtime. Point out that the words to today's Bible song show us how God can comfort us.

Bible Truth

Isaiah 12:1,2 says: "In that day you will say: 'I will praise you, O LORD. Although you were angry with me, your anger has turned away and you have comforted me. Surely God is my salvation; I will trust and not be afraid. The LORD, the LORD, is my strength and my song; he has become my salvation.' "

The prophet Isaiah, the writer of these words, knew that God hates sin and unbelief. Many times in the Bible, we read how God became very angry with his people when they sinned. We know that God hates our sin, and that can be very scary—scarier than a dark, stormy night. But just as flashlights and teddy bears can comfort us during scary nights, we know that God comforts us as well. He doesn't use teddy bears and flashlights. He uses the gift of salvation. He gave that gift to us by sending Jesus into the world to suffer, die, and rise.

Explain to the children how in the beautiful song found in Isaiah chapter 12—sometimes called "The First Song of Isaiah"—we hear how God is our salvation. That means that he has given us the sure hope of heaven through Jesus. Because of that, we never need to be afraid of God because of our sins. We need not be afraid of bad things in our world. We need not be afraid of anything!

Note how Isaiah also reminds us in his song to praise God for our salvation and that we can truly live with no fear.

Discussions and Applications

1. What are some things that might make people afraid?

2. What has God given to us that takes away our fear and gives us comfort?

3. What should we always remember to do when we think of God's gift of salvation?

CHAPEL TALKS FOR CHRISTIAN CHILDREN
JANUARY 19–23, 2004

Leader: As children of God, we worship the Lord our Savior.

Children: Let us unite our hearts and voices to praise his holy name.

SONG OF PRAISE O God from God, O Light from Light

John Julian

Johann Störls . . . Schlag-Gesang-Und Noten-Buch

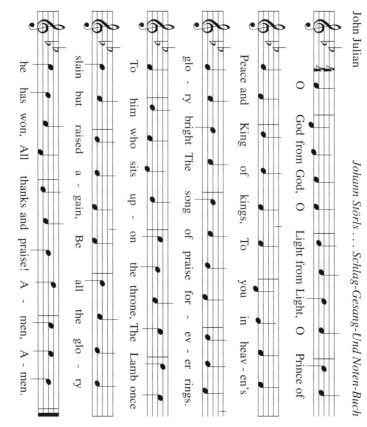

O God from God, O Light from Light, O Prince of Peace and King of kings, To you in heav - en's glo - ry bright The song of praise for - ev - er rings. To him who sits up - on the throne, The Lamb once slain but raised a - gain, Be all the glo - ry he has won, All thanks and praise! A - men, A - men.

Leader: Dear Jesus, we thank and praise you today for the wonderful gift of salvation that has been given to us. We know that because of your wonderful gift we can live with no fear. We also thank and praise you for the comfort you have given to us by promising us the sure hope of heaven. We pray this, Jesus, in your name. Amen.

HYMN I Am Trusting You, Lord Jesus

I am trusting you, Lord Jesus, Trusting only you, Trusting you for full salvation, Free and true.
I am trusting you for pardon; At your feet I bow, For your grace and tender mercy Trusting now.
I am trusting you for power; You can never fail. Words which you yourself shall give me Must prevail.
I am trusting you, Lord Jesus; Never let me fall. I am trusting you forever And for all.

PSALM 34

Leader: I will extol the LORD at all times;

Children: His praise will always be on my lips.

Leader: My soul will boast in the LORD;

Children: Let the afflicted hear and rejoice.

Leader: Glorify the LORD with me;

Children: Let us exalt his name together.

Leader: I sought the LORD, and he answered me;

Children: He delivered me from all my fears.

PRAYER REQUESTS

THE LORD'S PRAYER *(spoken together)*

OFFERINGS OF LOVE FOR JESUS

Leader: Now, children, go in peace. Live in harmony with one another. Serve the Lord with gladness.

The grace of our Lord ✝ Jesus Christ and the love of God and the fellowship of the Holy Spirit be with you all.

Children: Amen.

THE MESSAGE No Fear

In that day you will say: "I will praise you, O LORD. Although you were angry with me, your anger has turned away and you have comforted me. Surely God is my salvation; I will trust and not be afraid. The LORD, the LORD, is my strength and my song; he has become my salvation" (Isaiah 12:1,2).

Water Work and Water Play
Isaiah 12:3

Suggested for January 26–30, 2004

Visual Materials

- a small bucket filled with water
- a squirt gun or water toy
- a sponge used for washing

Object Lesson

Show the bucket of water and the sponge to the children. Ask: What do this bucket of water and sponge bring to mind? In what ways might we use these things? When you see the sponge with this bucket of water, you might think some hard work is coming. Show the squirt gun or water toy. Fill it up in the bucket of water. Ask: Now are you thinking that water means work? This squirt gun (water toy) reminds us that there are many ways of having fun with water. Playing with water can be a real joy! Explain that in this week's verse from the song found in chapter 12 of Isaiah, the group will see how Isaiah used water as a picture of joy—joy that comes from salvation.

Bible Truth

Isaiah 12:3 says, **"With joy you will draw water from the wells of salvation."**
Explain to the children how the Israelites didn't necessarily find joy in drawing water from the wells outside their villages and towns. It was hard work. That's why Isaiah's picture in this song at first seems strange. Ask: When we listen to our verse today, what kind of well does Isaiah say this water comes from? When the Israelites draw this water, what will be their attitude or mood as they work?

Explain to the children that the picture in this song is a picture of the joy we have because we are saved. We have faith that the Holy Spirit has given to us. Sometimes that faith dims and becomes weak. When God's Word reminds us of the salvation we have through Jesus, that Word "waters" our faith, and it becomes strong again. In joy we see that we are God's children through faith.

God wants us to be happy. He wants us to be filled with joy. He makes sure we can be filled with joy by reminding us of our salvation—our sure hope of heaven. Remind the children that Jesus' suffering, death, and resurrection won for them that salvation. Knowing that truth gives true joy!

Discussions and Applications

1. Give some examples of "water work." Give examples of "water play."

2. What does God's Word "water" in our lives?

3. When our faith is "watered," we are reminded of the joy that comes from knowing what?

CHAPEL TALKS FOR CHRISTIAN CHILDREN

JANUARY 26-30, 2004

Leader: As children of God, we worship the Lord our Savior.

Children: **Let us unite our hearts and voices to praise his holy name.**

SONG OF PRAISE O God from God, O Light from Light

John Julian   *Johann Störls . . . Schlag-Gesang-Und Noten-Buch*

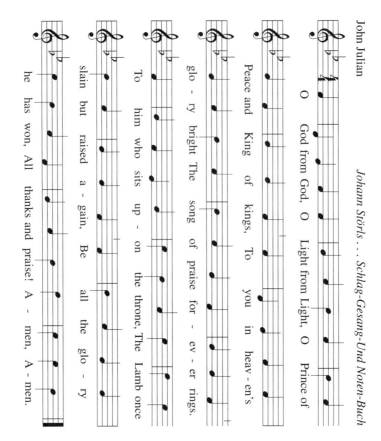

O God from God, O Light from Light, O Prince of Peace and King of kings, To you in heav - en's glo - ry bright The song of praise for - ev - er rings. To him who sits up - on the throne, The Lamb once slain but raised a - gain, Be all the glo - ry he has won, All thanks and praise! A - men, A - men.

THE MESSAGE Water Work and Water Play

With joy you will draw water from the wells of salvation (Isaiah 12:3).

Leader: Dear Jesus, because you suffered, died, and rose again, we now have joy knowing that we are saved. Thank you for this wonderful gift! Help us to keep this joy in our hearts and to share this joy with others by using your

---

Word to "water" our faith. We pray this, Lord Jesus, in your name. Amen.

HYMN Speak, O Savior; I Am Listening

Speak, O Savior; I am list'ning,
As a servant to his lord.
Let me show respect and honor
To your holy, precious Word,
That each day, my whole life through,
I may serve and follow you.
Let your Word e'er be my pleasure
And my heart's most precious treasure.

PSALM 42

Leader: As the deer pants for streams of water,

Children: **So my soul pants for you, O God.**

Leader: My soul thirsts for God, for the living God.

Children: **When can I go and meet with God?**

Leader: Why are you downcast, O my soul?

Children: **Why so disturbed within me?**

Leader: Put your hope in God,

Children: **For I will yet praise him, my Savior and my God.**

PRAYER REQUESTS

THE LORD'S PRAYER (*spoken together*)

OFFERINGS OF LOVE FOR JESUS

Leader: Now, children, go in peace. Live in harmony with one another. Serve the Lord with gladness.

The grace of our Lord ✝ Jesus Christ and the love of God and the fellowship of the Holy Spirit be with you all.

Children: **Amen.**

Get the Word Out
Isaiah 12:4

Suggested For February 2–6, 2004

Visual Materials

- a newspaper
- a magazine
- a small radio

Object Lesson

Show the three listed items. Tell the children to list ways each of the items are used in our world. Through discussion, direct the children to conclude that all three items can be used to give people information or tell people news, but they all do so in different ways. Ask: What great news do we as Christians have that we should share with the world? Explain that in the song that Isaiah wrote in chapter 12 of his book, he tells us about the salvation we have because of God's love for us. He also tells us that we should share that wonderful news with all nations!

Bible Truth

Isaiah 12:4 says, **"In that day you will say: 'Give thanks to the Lord, call on his name; make known among the nations what he has done, and proclaim that his name is exalted.' "**

Isaiah's song is such a joyful song! He writes and we sing about the gift of salvation won for us by Jesus' suffering, death, and resurrection. Isaiah realized, and so should we, that this news is not to be kept secret. We shouldn't hide this news inside of us. We need to share the news with as many people as we can. Have the children note that Isaiah tells us to share with the nations all God has done. Ask: What words did Jesus use to tell his disciples to share God's Word with all nations?

Newspapers, magazines, and radios can all be used in different ways to share news with the world. We also have different ways to share the news of our salvation. We can do it through the words we use when we are with friends. We can show we're Christians through our actions. We can sing songs like "The First Song of Isaiah" and share our faith through music. We know that no matter how we share God's Word and the news of our salvation with others, God will bless our efforts.

Isaiah also shows how we can be sure that God will bless our work of getting the Word out. He tells us to "call on God's name." Ask: What does calling on God mean? We should remember to pray that God allows the message of his salvation to be spread to all nations. When that happens, he will be exalted! Ask: What does *exalted* mean? When God is exalted, he becomes number one in our hearts. Let's continue to share his Word. Encourage the children to continue—with God's help—to keep God number one and to work hard as they get the Word out!

Discussions and Applications

1. Why is it so important to tell others about God's message of salvation?

2. What are some ways we can share God's Word?

3. What happens when God's Word is shared with the nations?

CHAPEL TALKS FOR CHRISTIAN CHILDREN
FEBRUARY 2–6, 2004

Leader: As children of God, we worship the Lord our Savior.

Children: Let us unite our hearts and voices to praise his holy name.

SONG OF PRAISE O God from God, O Light from Light

John Julian

Johann Störls . . . Schlag-Gesang-Und Noten-Buch

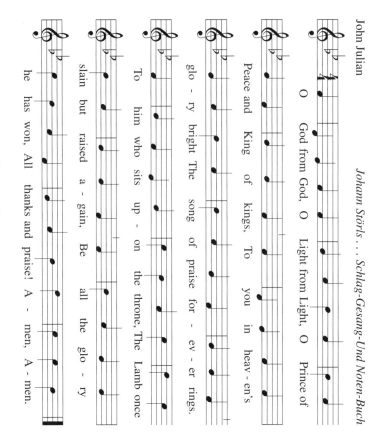

O God from God, O Light from Light, O Prince of

Peace and King of kings, To you in heav - en's

glo - ry bright The song of praise for - ev - er rings.

To him who sits up - on the throne, The Lamb once

slain but raised a - gain, Be all the glo - ry

he has won, All thanks and praise! A - men, A - men.

THE MESSAGE Get the Word Out

In that day you will say: "Give thanks to the LORD, call on his name; make known among the nations what he has done, and proclaim that his name is exalted" (Isaiah 12:4).

Leader: Dear Jesus, we have been blessed by you with the wonderful gift of salvation. There are so many people in so many nations that do not know you. Help us through our words, our songs, and our actions to tell as

many people as we can about your wonderful message of salvation. We pray, dear Savior, in your name. Amen.

HYMN Spread, Oh, Spread the Mighty Word

Spread, oh, spread the mighty Word;
Spread the kingdom of the Lord
Ev'rywhere his breath has giv'n
Life to beings meant for heav'n.

Tell them how the Father's will
Made the world and keeps it still,
How his only Son he gave
All from sin and death to save.

Tell of our Redeemer's love,
Who forever does remove
By his holy sacrifice
All the guilt that on us lies.

Tell them of the Spirit giv'n
Now to guide us on to heav'n,
Strong and holy, just and true,
Working both to will and do.

PSALM 105

Leader: Give thanks to the LORD, call on his name;

Children: Make known among the nations what he has done.

Leader: Sing to him, sing praise to him;

Children: Tell of all his wonderful acts.

Leader: Glory in his holy name;

Children: Let the hearts of those who seek the LORD rejoice.

PRAYER REQUESTS

THE LORD'S PRAYER (spoken together)

OFFERINGS OF LOVE FOR JESUS

Leader: Now, children, go in peace. Live in harmony with one another. Serve the Lord with gladness.

The grace of our Lord ✝ Jesus Christ and the love of God and the fellowship of the Holy Spirit be with you all.

Children: Amen.

Sing and Shout
Isaiah 12:5,6

Suggested for February 9–13, 2004

Visual Materials

- pretend airline tickets

Object Lesson

Show the airline tickets to the children. Tell them—in a very boring and unexcited way—that the tickets are for a special flight to the best vacation spot in America. (Note: This "vacation spot" will vary, depending on your audience and the location of your church and school.) Ask: Did you notice anything unusual about the way I told you about the tickets? How do you think I should have told you? If you had tickets like this, do you think you would tell others about them? How would you tell them? Explain that the children would tell others with a huge amount of excitement! They might even shout the good news! Point out that in the song found in Isaiah chapter 12, we are told about some other good news that we are to shout to the world. That good news is the message of salvation—salvation that comes from Jesus and his love.

Bible Truth

Isaiah 12:5,6 says: **"Sing to the LORD, for he has done glorious things; let this be known to all the world. Shout aloud and sing for joy, people of Zion, for great is the Holy One of Israel among you."**

We know that when we have great news, we don't want to keep it to ourselves. We tell others, and we tell them with excitement. Isaiah had great news that he shares in his song, "The First Song of Isaiah." His great news is that God has done glorious things for us! The most glorious, most wonderful news is the gift of salvation God has given to us. God's Word tells us through Isaiah's song that we should sing and shout to the whole world about how great God is to us. We can do that in church when we sing during worship services. We can sing in our classrooms and choirs. We can sing songs that praise God for his wonderful love. When we sing like this, we are telling the world about him.

We can shout out the good news too! We can "shout" with our words and actions. By telling others about Jesus and by living in such a way that we show we love Jesus, we are "shouting" out the good news of our salvation to everyone.

As Christians, we have the great news that God loves us, and because of Jesus' suffering, death, and resurrection, we have salvation! There is no better news. Sing it out! Shout it out! Our great God has done glorious things!

Discussions and Applications

1. How do you share great news with someone else?

2. Why should we work hard at singing and shouting out the great news of the gospel?

CHAPEL TALKS FOR CHRISTIAN CHILDREN

FEBRUARY 9-13, 2004

Leader: As children of God, we worship the Lord our Savior.

Children: Let us unite our hearts and voices to praise his holy name.

SONG OF PRAISE O God from God, O Light from Light

John Julian

Johann Störls . . . Schlag-Gesang-Und Noten-Buch

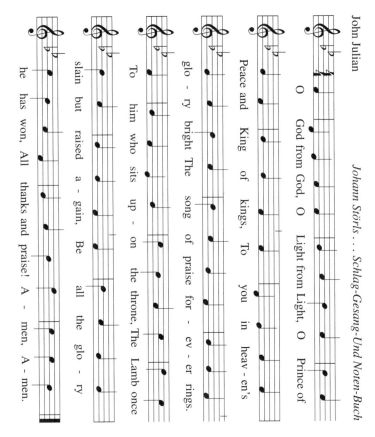

O God from God, O Light from Light, O Prince of

Peace and King of kings, To you in heav - en's

glo - ry bright The song of praise for - ev - er rings.

To him who sits up - on the throne, The Lamb once

slain but raised a - gain, Be all the glo - ry

he has won, All thanks and praise! A - men, A - men.

THE MESSAGE Sing and Shout

Sing to the LORD, for he has done glorious things; let this be known to all the world. Shout aloud and sing for joy, people of Zion, for great is the Holy One of Israel among you (Isaiah 12:5,6).

Leader: Dear Jesus, you have given us our salvation—that is the greatest gift and the greatest news we could ever receive. Thank you! Help us to sing and shout this news to everyone we can. Bless our words and actions as we follow the example of Isaiah by praising you and sharing your gospel message. In your name we pray. Amen.

HYMN Oh, That I Had a Thousand Voices

**Oh, that I had a thousand voices
To praise my God with thousand tongues!
My heart, which in the Lord rejoices,
Would then proclaim in grateful songs
To all, wherever I might be,
What great things God has done for me.**

**Lord, I will tell, while I am living,
Your love and grace with ev'ry breath
And greet each morning with thanksgiving
Until my heart is still in death,
And, when at last my lips grow cold,
Your praise shall in my sighs be told.**

PSALM 96

Leader: Sing to the LORD a new song;

Children: Sing to the LORD, all the earth.

Leader: Sing to the LORD, praise his name;

Children: Proclaim his salvation day after day.

Leader: Declare his glory among the nations,

Children: His marvelous deeds among all peoples.

PRAYER REQUESTS

THE LORD'S PRAYER (*spoken together*)

OFFERINGS OF LOVE FOR JESUS

Leader: Now, children, go in peace. Live in harmony with one another. Serve the Lord with gladness.

The grace of our Lord ✝ Jesus Christ and the love of God and the fellowship of the Holy Spirit be with you all.

Children: Amen.

The Comfort of Forgiveness
Isaiah 40:1,2

26

Suggested for February 16–20, 2004

Visual Materials

- a made-up bill or invoice with large letters that say "You Owe Us!"
- a made-up bill or invoice with large letters that say "Paid In Full!"

Object Lesson

Ask: How many of you enjoy getting mail? Show the "You Owe Us!" bill. Ask: How many of you would like to get this mail? Explain that getting mail can be fun, but sometimes bills like this take all the fun out of going to the mailbox. Show the "Paid In Full!" bill. Ask: What's the difference with this piece of mail? Would you like getting something like this in the mailbox? Point out that it tells us to forget about paying. Instead of writing checks to pay bills, we can sit down in a comfortable chair and relax. The bill is paid! Mention that today, in some verses of a song written by the prophet Isaiah, we learn about a different "bill" that has been paid and about a comfort much better than relaxing in a chair.

Bible Truth

Isaiah 40:1,2 says: **"Comfort, comfort my people, says your God. Speak tenderly to Jerusalem, and proclaim to her that her hard service has been completed, that her sin has been paid for, that she has received from the Lord 's hand double for all her sins."**

Like a big bill coming in the mailbox, sin can bring depression and sadness. God saw this depression and sadness in his people during the time of Isaiah. God needed to bring them comfort. He did so by having Isaiah write the verses of the song of comfort we just heard. In his song, Isaiah prophesied about something that was going to happen. Ask: What is prophecy? Do you know what Isaiah was prophesying about? Isaiah knew (because God told him) that some day Jesus would come as the Savior. When he would come, he would bring us a bill. The bill would say that we deserve death and hell because we are sinners. But Jesus would also bring a promise of comfort. This comfort is called forgiveness. Through Jesus' suffering, death, and resurrection, he marked our bill "Paid In Full!" He forgave our sins. He took them away completely. He gave and still gives us the comfort of knowing that we have nothing to fear because of our sins. They are gone forever. When we remember that our wonderful Savior paid for our sins and gives us this great comfort, we will want to thank and praise him with our songs, words, and actions.

Discussions and Applications

1. What kind of "bill," or debt, did we once owe?

2. Who paid our bill? How did he do this?

3. What should we do to show our appreciation for having our "bill" forgiven?

CHAPEL TALKS FOR CHRISTIAN CHILDREN
FEBRUARY 16–20, 2004

Leader: As children of God, we worship the Lord our Savior.

Children: **Let us unite our hearts and voices to praise his holy name.**

SONG OF PRAISE O God from God, O Light from Light

John Julian

Johann Störls . . . Schlag-Gesang-Und Noten-Buch

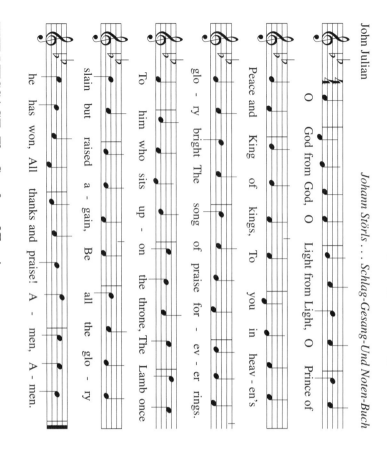

O God from God, O Light from Light, O Prince of
Peace and King of kings, To you in heav-en's
glo-ry bright The song of praise for - ev - er rings.
To him who sits up - on the throne, The Lamb once
slain but raised a - gain, Be all the glo - ry
he has won, All thanks and praise! A - men, A - men.

THE MESSAGE The Comfort of Forgiveness

Comfort, comfort my people, says your God. Speak tenderly to Jerusalem, and proclaim to her that her hard service has been completed, that her sin has been paid for, that she has received from the LORD's hand double for all her sins (Isaiah 40:1,2).

Leader: Dear Jesus, a long time ago Isaiah prophesied that you would come into this world to carry out your plan of salvation. We enjoy the comfort of forgiveness because you paid our debt of sin. Help us to show you—every day—through our words and our actions how much we love you for being our Savior. We pray this, Jesus, in your name. Amen.

HYMN Comfort, Comfort All My People

"Comfort, comfort all my people;
Speak of peace," so says our God.
"Comfort those who sit in darkness,
Groaning from their sorrows' load.
Speak to all Jerusalem
Of the peace that waits for them;
Tell them that their sins I cover,
That their warfare now is over."

All their sins our God will pardon,
Blotting out each dark misdeed;
All that well deserve his anger
He no more will see or heed.
They have suffered many a day;
Now their griefs have passed away.
God will change their aching sadness
Into ever-springing gladness.

PSALM 85

Leader: You showed favor to your land, O LORD;

Children: **You restored the fortunes of Jacob.**

Leader: You forgave the iniquity of your people

Children: **And covered all their sins.**

Leader: You set aside all your wrath

Children: **And turned from your fierce anger.**

PRAYER REQUESTS

THE LORD'S PRAYER *(spoken together)*

OFFERINGS OF LOVE FOR JESUS

Leader: Now, children, go in peace. Live in harmony with one another. Serve the Lord with gladness.

The grace of our Lord ✝ Jesus Christ and the love of God and the fellowship of the Holy Spirit be with you all.

Children: **Amen.**

Removing the Barricade
Isaiah 40:3-5

27

Suggested For February 23–27, 2004

Visual Materials

- some type of barricade or obstacle (a picture or a plastic model from a toy car set)

Object Lesson

Show the barricade to the children. Ask: What is something like this meant to do? Explain that it's meant to keep someone or something from entering an area or from moving forward. Ask: Why might some barricades be stronger than others? Tell the children the barricades have to be strong if they are meant to keep strong or powerful things from entering. Point out that in the reading today, Isaiah talks about barricades that have been removed.

Bible Truth

Isaiah 40:3-5 says: **"A voice of one calling: 'In the desert prepare the way for the LORD; make straight in the wilderness a highway for our God. Every valley shall be raised up, every mountain and hill made low; the rough ground shall become level, the rugged places a plain. And the glory of the LORD will be revealed, and all mankind together will see it. For the mouth of the LORD has spoken.' "**

Ask: What kind of barricades does Isaiah speak of in the words of his song? He speaks of deep valleys, high mountains, and rough, rugged places. Notice what has happened to these barricades. The deep valleys are raised up while the mountains are lowered to the ground. The rough and rugged places are made smooth and level. These barricades and obstacles that Isaiah writes about are actually pictures of sin. Sin is the barricade that stands in our way as we prepare for the coming of our Lord. These barricades are removed when we repent of our sins and believe in Jesus as our Savior! That's what John the Baptist talked about when he was working to prepare people for Jesus' coming. He talked about repentance.

Ask: What part of Isaiah's song makes us think about John the Baptist? "In the desert prepare the way." John knew, and we know to, that in order to be ready for Jesus' coming, we need to repent of our sins and believe that Jesus has forgiven them. When Jesus does come again, he'll see us covered with his forgiveness—the forgiveness he gave us for free. Let's rejoice that Jesus has removed this barricade from our lives!

Discussion and Applications

1. What type of barricade does the devil place in our way to keep us away from our Lord?

2. How did Jesus remove this barricade?

CHAPEL TALKS FOR CHRISTIAN CHILDREN
FEBRUARY 23–27, 2004

Leader: As children of God, we worship the Lord our Savior.

Children: **Let us unite our hearts and voices to praise his holy name.**

SONG OF PRAISE O God from God, O Light from Light

John Julian   Johann Störls . . . Schlag-Gesang-Und Noten-Buch

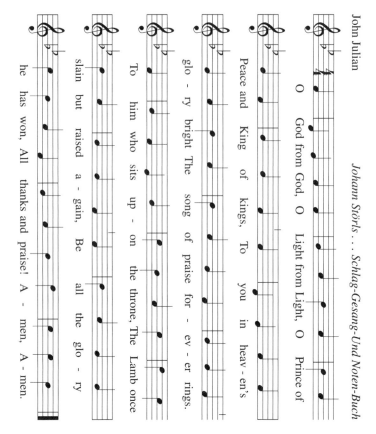

O God from God, O Light from Light, O Prince of

Peace and King of kings, To you in heav-en's

glo - ry bright The song of praise for - ev - er rings.

To him who sits up - on the throne, The Lamb once

slain but raised a - gain, Be all the glo - ry

he has won, All thanks and praise! A - men. A - men.

Leader: Dear Jesus, I am very sorry for the times I have sinned against you. Please forgive the sins I commit, and remove the barricade of sin from my life. Thank you for giving me the assurance that my sins are completely forgiven because of your suffering, death, and resurrection. In your name I pray. Amen.

HYMN Comfort, Comfort All My People

John the Baptist's voice is crying
In the desert far and near,
Calling people to repentance
For the kingdom now is here.
Oh, that warning cry obey!
Now prepare for God a way;
Let the valleys rise to meet him
And the hills bow down to greet him.

Straighten out the crooked highway;
Make the rougher places plain.
Let your hearts be true and humble,
Ready for his holy reign.
For the glory of the Lord
Now o'er earth is spread abroad,
And all flesh shall see the token
That his word is never broken.

PSALM 51

Leader: Have mercy on me, O God,

Children: **According to your unfailing love;**

Leader: According to your great compassion

Children: **Blot out my transgressions.**

Leader: Wash away all my iniquity

Children: **And cleanse me from my sin.**

PRAYER REQUESTS

THE LORD'S PRAYER (spoken together)

OFFERINGS OF LOVE FOR JESUS

Leader: Now, children, go in peace. Live in harmony with one another. Serve the Lord with gladness.

The grace of our Lord ✝ Jesus Christ and the love of God and the fellowship of the Holy Spirit be with you all.

Children: **Amen.**

THE MESSAGE Removing the Barricade

A voice of one calling: "In the desert prepare the way for the LORD; make straight in the wilderness a highway for our God. Every valley shall be raised up, every mountain and hill made low; the rough ground shall become level, the rugged places a plain. And the glory of the LORD will be revealed, and all mankind together will see it. For the mouth of the LORD has spoken" (Isaiah 40:3-5).

Down in the Pits

28

Psalm 130:1-4

Suggested for March 1–5, 2004

Visual Materials

- a picture of a cave (the more intimidating, the better)

Object Lesson

Many people like to take vacations. For some, the more unusual the vacation, the better. Show the picture of the cave. Ask: Does this look like a good vacation spot? Explain that for some people, exploring this cave might be a wonderful adventure. For others, the thought of getting lost deep in the pits of this cave is very scary. Mention that today the group will take a look at some verses from Psalm 130 that compare the human sinful condition to being lost deep in the depths of a cave, or a pit. Ask: Will we stay lost, or will God lead us out?

Bible Truth

Psalm 130:1-4 says: **"Out of the depths I cry to you, O Lord; O Lord, hear my voice. Let your ears be attentive to my cry for mercy. If you, O Lord, kept a record of sins, O Lord, who could stand? But with you there is forgiveness; therefore you are feared."**

The verses of this psalm are actually verses of a song written long ago. That's what psalms are—songs that the children of Israel once sang and songs that we still sing today.

The writer of this psalm is in a tight spot. He is stuck in the depths of his sin. Ask: What picture did we use earlier as a picture of "depths"? He is crying to God for mercy. He knows that he has no chance for rescue from this pit if he tries to save himself. He knows that if God kept a record of sins, a book of all the wrongs we do, the writer would never be brought up out of these depths—he'd actually sink further down.

Ask: What rescues us from sin? God's forgiveness is the key. We know that because Jesus suffered, died, and rose again, we have the blessing of forgiveness. Our sins are gone! We are raised up out of the pit from which we cry out, and we are placed onto the firm ground of salvation—all because Jesus loves us so much! Our cries for help become songs of praise! We were down in the pits of sin, but now we are rescued through the forgiveness earned for us by Jesus. It's him we praise!

Discussions and Applications

1. When the psalmist wrote today's psalm, to what did he compare our sinful condition?

2. How did Jesus rescue us from "the pits"?

3. What should we want to do, knowing that we have forgiveness?

CHAPEL TALKS FOR CHRISTIAN CHILDREN

MARCH 1–5, 2004

Leader: As children of God, we worship the Lord our Savior.

Children: Let us unite our hearts and voices to praise his holy name.

SONG OF PRAISE Christ, the Life of All the Living

Ernst C. Homburg
tr. Catherine Winkworth

Das grosse Cantional

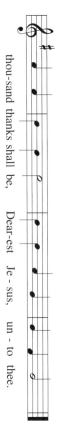

Christ, the Life of all the liv - ing, Christ, the Death of

death, our foe, Who, thy - self for me once giv - ing

To the dark - est depths of woe— Through thy suf - f'rings,

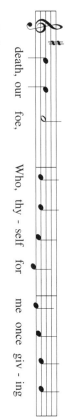

death, and mer - it I e - ter - nal life in - her - it. Thou-sand,

thou-sand thanks shall be, Dear-est Je - sus, un - to thee.

THE MESSAGE Down in the Pits

Out of the depths I cry to you, O LORD; O Lord, hear my voice. Let your ears be attentive to my cry for mercy. If you, O LORD, kept a record of sins, O Lord, who could stand? But with you there is forgiveness; therefore you are feared (Psalm 130:1-4).

Leader: Dear Jesus, sin can really bring us down. It makes us feel like we are trapped in the deepest pit or the darkest cave. But you came into this world to take away our sins

---

and to give to us the gift of forgiveness. For this, we thank and praise you each and every day. We pray this in your name. Amen.

HYMN Savior, When in Dust to You

Savior, when in dust to you
Low we bow in homage due,
When, repentant, to the skies
Scarce we lift our weeping eyes;
Oh, by all your pains and woe
Suffered once for us below,
Bending from your throne on high,
Hear our penitential cry!

By your helpless infant years,
By your life of want and tears,
By your days of deep distress
In the savage wilderness,
By the dread, mysterious hour
Of th' insulting tempter's pow'r,
Turn, oh, turn a fav'ring eye,
Hear our penitential cry!

PSALM 130

Leader: Out of the depths I cry to you, O LORD;

Children: O Lord, hear my voice.

Leader: Let your ears be attentive

Children: To my cry for mercy.

Leader: If you, O LORD, kept a record of sins,

Children: O Lord, who could stand?

Leader: But with you there is forgiveness;

Children: Therefore you are feared.

PRAYER REQUESTS

THE LORD'S PRAYER (spoken together)

OFFERINGS OF LOVE FOR JESUS

Leader: Now, children, go in peace. Live in harmony with one another. Serve the Lord with gladness.

The grace of our Lord ☩ Jesus Christ and the love of God and the fellowship of the Holy Spirit be with you all.

Children: Amen.

Hope in the Lord
Psalm 130:5-8

29

Suggested for March 8–12, 2004

Visual Materials

- a sign that reads "Please Wait Here"

Object Lesson

Show the children the sign. Ask them to read it out loud. Ask: Where might you find a sign like this? Listen to different responses. Ask: Is it ever easy to wait? Have the children come up with times when waiting might be easy. Ask: Is it ever hard to wait? Once again, listen for responses that tell when waiting might be very hard. Make this conclusion: Waiting is different for everyone. For some, waiting is never easy. For others, waiting is no trouble at all. In our psalm verses for today, the writer is waiting for something very important. He doesn't say it's easy waiting, he doesn't say it's hard waiting either. Suggest that the children listen to what his waiting is all about.

Bible Truth

Psalm 130:5-8 says: **"I wait for the Lord, my soul waits, and in his word I put my hope. My soul waits for the Lord more than watchmen wait for the morning, more than watchmen wait for the morning. O Israel, put your hope in the Lord, for with the Lord is unfailing love and with him is full redemption. He himself will redeem Israel from all their sins."**

The writer of this psalm—one of the songs from the hymnbook used by the children of Israel—tells us he is waiting for the Lord. As he waited, he waited with something. He waited with hope. The writer compares his waiting to the watchmen who would sit on top of city walls and keep their eyes open for trouble. That may have been long, hard waiting for them. However, they knew that once morning came, the trouble that night can bring would be long behind them. Just as these watchmen waited for the peace and comfort of morning, so the writer waited for the peace and comfort that comes from the Lord.

We have that same peace and comfort. It is peace and comfort that come from something the psalm writer called "full redemption." Ask: Does anyone know what *redemption* means? When we are redeemed, we are ransomed, or bought back, from the evil that once had hold of us. Ask: What is this evil? Because we are redeemed, we know our sins are forgiven. That brings peace and comfort. The devil no longer has hold on us.

Ask: Is this redemption something that we will have someday but do not have yet? This redemption and forgiveness are ours—now! They became ours when Jesus suffered, died, and rose again. Our waiting is over, and we now have sure hope—of life forever in heaven! That is true peace and comfort!

Discussions and Applications

1. From what has the Lord redeemed us? Do we have this blessing now, or do we have to wait for it?

2. How did the Lord redeem us?

3. How does the Lord's saving work of redemption give us peace and comfort?

CHAPEL TALKS FOR CHRISTIAN CHILDREN

MARCH 8-12, 2004

Leader: As children of God, we worship the Lord our Savior.

Children: Let us unite our hearts and voices to praise his holy name.

SONG OF PRAISE Christ, the Life of All the Living

Ernst C. Homburg
tr. Catherine Winkworth

Das grosse Cantional

Christ, the Life of all the liv - ing, Christ, the Death of

death, our foe, Who, thy - self for me once giv - ing

To the dark - est depths of woe— Through thy suf - f'rings,

death, and mer - it I e - ter - nal life in - her - it. Thou-sand,

thou-sand thanks shall be, Dear-est Je - sus, un - to thee.

Leader: Dear Jesus, thank you for giving us the sure hope of heaven by redeeming us and forgiving our sins. Because of your love for us, our waiting is over. We know that your love for us is so great that you came to suffer, die, and rise again to win our salvation. Thank you for this gift that brings peace and comfort. In your name we pray. Amen.

HYMN Come, O Precious Ransom, Come

**Come, O precious Ransom, come,
Only Hope for sinful mortals!
Come, O Savior of the world!
Open are to you all portals.
Come, your beauty let us view;
Anxiously we wait for you.**

**Enter now my waiting heart,
Glorious King and Lord most holy.
Dwell in me and ne'er depart,
Though I am but poor and lowly.
Ah, what riches will be mine
When you are my guest divine!**

PSALM 130

Leader: I wait for the LORD, my soul waits,
Children: And in his word I put my hope.

Leader: My soul waits for the Lord more than watchmen wait for the morning,

Children: More than watchmen wait for the morning.

Leader: O Israel, put your hope in the LORD,
Children: For with the LORD is unfailing love

Leader: And with him is full redemption.
Children: He himself will redeem Israel from all their sins.

PRAYER REQUESTS

THE LORD'S PRAYER (*spoken together*)

OFFERINGS OF LOVE FOR JESUS

Leader: Now, children, go in peace. Live in harmony with one another. Serve the Lord with gladness.

The grace of our Lord + Jesus Christ and the love of God and the fellowship of the Holy Spirit be with you all.

Children: Amen.

THE MESSAGE Hope in the Lord

I wait for the LORD, my soul waits, and in his word I put my hope. My soul waits for the Lord more than watchmen wait for the morning, more than watchmen wait for the morning. O Israel, put your hope in the LORD, for with the LORD is unfailing love and with him is full redemption. He himself will redeem Israel from all their sins (Psalm 130:5-8).

The Common Man
Isaiah 53:1,2

30

Suggested for March 15–19, 2004

Visual Materials

- a photograph of an ordinary man—not a celebrity or a recognizable face

Object Lesson

Show the picture. Ask: Does anyone know this man? Point out that he's not famous. He's not a star or an athlete. Suggest that he's just an ordinary man. Ask: Do you see anything special about this man in his picture? Again, suggest there is nothing special or extraordinary. He's just a common man.

Choose a student from the group. Ask the children: How would the answers you just gave be different if the picture was of this student's dad? Make the point that the man wouldn't just be ordinary—especially to this student. He'd be someone they know. He wouldn't be just a common man.

Explain that in today's reading—taken from a song written by the prophet Isaiah—the group will hear that Jesus was to come into the world as a common man. His appearance, his "look," would be nothing special. However, to those who know Jesus, he is very special.

Bible Truth

Isaiah 53:1,2 says: **"Who has believed our message and to whom has the arm of the LORD been revealed? He grew up before him like a tender shoot, and like a root out of dry ground. He had no beauty or majesty to attract us to him, nothing in his appearance that we should desire him."**

Jesus came into this world as the God-man. Ask: What does *God-man* mean? Jesus is true God and true man at the very same time. Ask: When people living during Jesus' time looked at Jesus, what did they see? They saw a common man. Isaiah said that this would be the case. He said there would be nothing in Jesus' appearance that would stand out, that would attract followers.

Ask: How do we explain the followers that Jesus did have? Did they see more than just a common man? Point out that they did—and so do we! We see the God-man, who had a mission. He came into this world to save sinners. All of us were lost in sin. Jesus changed that. The suffering, death, and resurrection of the God-man give us the sure hope of salvation. As both man and God, he was able to die for our sins, and he was able to defeat death and come out of the grave.

Jesus is true man. Jesus is true God. Jesus as the God-man won salvation for us. The fact that the God-man is our Savior gives us a joy that will last an eternity! It's important to remember to thank and praise Jesus for his work and for the gift of salvation he gave to us.

Discussions and Applications

1. Jesus is the *God-man.* What do we mean by that term?

2. What was the God-man's mission?

3. How did Jesus accomplish his mission? What should our reaction be to the work Jesus completed?

CHAPEL TALKS FOR CHRISTIAN CHILDREN

MARCH 15-19, 2004

Leader: As children of God, we worship the Lord our Savior.

Children: **Let us unite our hearts and voices to praise his holy name.**

SONG OF PRAISE Christ, the Life of All the Living

Ernst C. Homburg
tr. Catherine Winkworth

Das grosse Cantional

Christ, the Life of all the liv - ing, Christ, the Death of

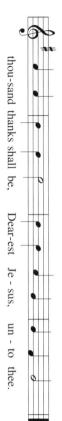

death, our foe, Who, thy - self for me once giv - ing

To the dark - est depths of woe— Through thy suf - f'rings,

death, and mer - it I e - ter - nal life in - her - it. Thou - sand,

thou - sand thanks shall be, Dear - est Je - sus, un - to thee.

THE MESSAGE The Common Man

Who has believed our message and to whom has the arm of the LORD been revealed? He grew up before him like a tender shoot, and like a root out of dry ground. He had no beauty or majesty to attract us to him, nothing in his appearance that we should desire him (Isaiah 53:1,2).

Leader: Dear Jesus, you came into this world as the God-man to carry out your mission. That mission was to save us from an eternity in hell. Thank you, Jesus, for the saving work that you have done. Thank you for the sure hope of heaven. Help us to remember every day to give you the glory, honor, and praise you deserve. In your name we pray this. Amen.

HYMN O Dearest Jesus

O dearest Jesus, what law have you broken
That such sharp sentence should on you be spoken?
Of what great crime have you to make confession—
What dark transgression?

The sinless Son of God must die in sadness;
The sinful child of man may live in gladness;
We forfeited our lives, yet are acquitted—
God is committed.

PSALM 98

Leader: Sing to the LORD a new song,

Children: **For he has done marvelous things;**

Leader: His right hand and his holy arm

Children: **Have worked salvation for him.**

Leader: The LORD has made his salvation known

Children: **And revealed his righteousness to the nations.**

PRAYER REQUESTS

THE LORD'S PRAYER *(spoken together)*

OFFERINGS OF LOVE FOR JESUS

Leader: Now, children, go in peace. Live in harmony with one another. Serve the Lord with gladness.

The grace of our Lord ✝ Jesus Christ and the love of God and the fellowship of the Holy Spirit be with you all.

Children: **Amen.**

Jesus Hated—For Me!
Isaiah 53:3

31

Suggested For March 22–26, 2004

Visual Materials

- something to represent a restaurant menu (not from an establishment the children know)

Object Lesson

Show the menu to the children, and tell them that you are going to pick a meal for them. Encourage a reaction as you read a list of foods that would be on their lists of "hated" foods. Liver, asparagus, cauliflower, and more might come to mind. Ask: Why are you making faces? Aren't these foods you would order? Work the word *hate* into your conversation with the children.

Clarify that *hate* is a strong word. It's a word that we might use to describe foods, even those that are good for us. Ask: Is it ever a word we would use when we talk about people? Is it ever a word that should be used when we talk about Jesus?

Explain that in the verse today—a verse from a song that Isaiah wrote many years ago—the group will see that people hated Jesus. Encourage the children to learn what that hatred caused to happen.

Bible Truth

Isaiah 53:3 says: **"He was despised and rejected by men, a man of sorrows, and familiar with suffering. Like one from whom men hide their faces he was despised, and we esteemed him not."**

In his song, Isaiah foretold the future. Ask: What do we call the work of foretelling the future as the men of God did in the Old Testament? Isaiah was prophesying, and his prophecy was a sad one. It talks about the fact that when Jesus would come into this world, men would hate him. Isaiah used the words *despised* and *rejected.* Jesus would be hated so much that men would want to hide their faces from his, just as you hid your faces from the foods we read earlier from our menu.

The hatred these people had became so strong that they actually killed Jesus. Their hatred led to murder. As horrible as that sounds, however, it was what Jesus had planned. He knew he would be hated. He knew he would be killed. He knew all this, and yet he still came to this earth. Through his death, we have salvation. When those men killed Jesus, he willingly died to take away their sins and our sins as well. The great news is this: Jesus didn't stay dead! He came out of his grave alive to give us salvation. People hate him. He loves us. He loves us so much he went to the cross for us. That is a Savior! That is our Savior!

Today, there are some who still hate Jesus. They hate him because they don't know him as their Savior. Let's do all we can to share the great news that Jesus died and rose to win salvation for everyone! Let's share the love of Jesus so the hate people have in their hearts can disappear forever.

Discussions and Applications

1. Name some things Jesus knew would happen when he came into this world.

2. When Jesus died and then rose from the dead, what did he win for us?

3. What should we do with the great news of salvation?

CHAPEL TALKS FOR CHRISTIAN CHILDREN

MARCH 22–26, 2004

Leader: As children of God, we worship the Lord our Savior.

Children: **Let us unite our hearts and voices to praise his holy name.**

SONG OF PRAISE Christ, the Life of All the Living

Das grosse Cantional

Ernst C. Homburg
tr. Catherine Winkworth

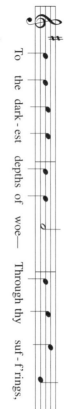
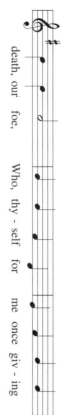

Christ, the Life of all the liv-ing, Christ, the Death of

death, our foe, Who, thy-self for me once giv-ing

To the dark-est depths of woe— Through thy suf-f'rings,

death, and mer-it I e-ter-nal life in-her-it. Thou-sand,

thou-sand thanks shall be, Dear-est Je-sus, un-to thee.

THE MESSAGE Jesus Hated—For Me!

He was despised and rejected by men, a man of sorrows, and familiar with suffering. Like one from whom men hide their faces he was despised, and we esteemed him not (Isaiah 53:3).

Leader: Dear Jesus, I have nothing but love for you in my heart. I am sad when I think about the people who hated you and killed you, but I know you went through that suffering for me. Thank you for the wonderful love that led you to the cross. Thank you for giving me salvation. Help me to take your love to others so that the hatred they have in their hearts can be erased forever. Thank you, Jesus, for being my Savior. In your name I pray. Amen.

HYMN Hail, O Once-Despised Jesus

Hail, O once-despised Jesus! Hail, O Galilean King!
You have suffered to release us, Hope to give and peace
to bring.
Hail, O universal Savior, Bearer of our sin and shame;
By your merits we find favor; Life is given through
your name.

Paschal Lamb, by God appointed, All our sins on you
were laid;
By almighty love anointed, You have full atonement
made.
Ev'ry sin has been forgiven Through the power of your
blood;
Open is the gate of heaven; We are reconciled to God.

PSALM 22

Leader: My God, my God, why have you forsaken me?

Children: **Why are you so far from saving me?**

Leader: O my God, I cry out by day,

Children: **But you do not answer.**

Leader: I am a worm and not a man,

Children: **Scorned by men and despised by the people.**

Leader: Yet you are enthroned as the Holy One;

Children: **You are the praise of Israel.**

PRAYER REQUESTS

THE LORD'S PRAYER *(spoken together)*

OFFERINGS OF LOVE FOR JESUS

Leader: Now, children, go in peace. Live in harmony with one another. Serve the Lord with gladness.

The grace of our Lord ✝ Jesus Christ and the love of God and the fellowship of the Holy Spirit be with you all.

Children: **Amen.**

He Took Our Punishment
Isaiah 53:4,5

Suggested for March 29–April 2, 2004

Visual Materials

- a dictionary
- a pad of paper and a pencil

Object Lesson

Explain to the children that you want to show what some teachers use as tools. Explain that the dictionary can be used as a tool in learning new words. The pencil and paper can be used to practice writing, to take notes, and more.

Ask: Can you think of something else these items might be used to accomplish? Point out that they can be used as punishment tools. Encourage the children to imagine a misbehaving student—not any of them, of course—that gets in trouble and must start copying the dictionary. What a task! Just before this poor student starts copying, a friend comes in and says: "Go play. I'll copy it for you." What a friend! Explain that he takes the punishment even though he didn't do the wrong.

Mention that in the verse today, the children will hear that they really do have such a friend. This friend took their punishment and suffered it for them. That friend's name is Jesus.

Bible Truth

Isaiah 53:4,5 says: **"Surely he took up our infirmities and carried our sorrows, yet we considered him stricken by God, smitten by him, and afflicted. But he was pierced for our transgressions, he was crushed for our iniquities; the punishment that brought us peace was upon him, and by his wounds we are healed."**

The prophet Isaiah is talking about Jesus in the verses we just read. He is telling how Jesus would suffer and die. List some of the horrible words that describe what would happen to Jesus: *stricken, smitten, afflicted, pierced, crushed.* Ask: When did all these terrible things happen to Jesus? When Jesus was crucified, he suffered in ways we can't even begin to imagine.

The amazing thing is this: Jesus suffered and died this way for us! Over and over again, Isaiah says that Jesus suffered our punishment. He was pierced and crushed for our sins! Ask: What would make Jesus do this? It was out of love that Jesus went through such a horrible ordeal. It was love for us that made him take our punishment. Ask: What do we call Jesus because of this love? Jesus is our Savior. He saved us from the punishment that we should suffer in hell forever. Now, because Jesus took our punishment, we know that we will live forever with him in heaven.

Savior is a beautiful word. It's a word you might look up sometime in your dictionary. It's a word that will always remind us of what Jesus did for us. He took our punishment and gave us heaven!

Discussions and Applications

1. What horrible things did Jesus suffer when he went to the cross?
2. Why did he suffer such things?
3. What do we call Jesus because of the love he has for us?

CHAPEL TALKS FOR CHRISTIAN CHILDREN

MARCH 29–APRIL 2, 2004

Leader: As children of God, we worship the Lord our Savior.

Children: **Let us unite our hearts and voices to praise his holy name.**

SONG OF PRAISE Christ, the Life of All the Living

Ernst C. Homburg
tr. Catherine Winkworth

Das grosse Cantional

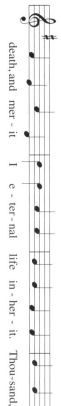

Christ, the Life of all the liv - ing, Christ, the Death of

death, our foe, Who, thy - self for me once giv - ing

To the dark - est depths of woe— Through thy suf - f'rings,

death, and mer - it I e - ter - nal life in - her - it. Thou-sand,

thou-sand thanks shall be, Dear-est Je - sus, un - to thee.

THE MESSAGE He Took Our Punishment

Surely he took up our infirmities and carried our sorrows, yet we considered him stricken by God, smitten by him, and afflicted. But he was pierced for our transgressions, he was crushed for our iniquities; the punishment that brought us peace was upon him, and by his wounds we are healed (Isaiah 53:4,5).

Dear Jesus, my Savior, thank you for going to the cross in my place. I know you did this for me because you love

me. Let me show my love to you as well by giving you praise, honor, and glory. In your name I pray. Amen.

HYMN Stricken, Smitten, and Afflicted

Stricken, smitten, and afflicted,
See him dying on the tree!
'Tis the Christ, by man rejected;
Yes, my soul, 'tis he, 'tis he.
'Tis the long-expected Prophet,
David's Son, yet David's Lord;
Proofs I see sufficient of it: '
Tis the true and faithful Word.

Here we have a firm foundation,
Here the refuge of the lost;
Christ's the rock of our salvation,
His the name of which we boast.
Lamb of God, for sinners wounded,
Sacrifice to cancel guilt—
None shall ever be confounded
Who on him their hope have built.

PSALM 22

Leader: My God, my God, why have you forsaken me?

Children: **Why are you so far from saving me?**

Leader: I can count all my bones;

Children: **People stare and gloat over me.**

Leader: They divide my garments among them

Children: **And cast lots for my clothing.**

Leader: But you, O LORD, be not far off;

Children: **O my Strength, come quickly to help me.**

PRAYER REQUESTS

THE LORD'S PRAYER (*spoken together*)

OFFERINGS OF LOVE FOR JESUS

Leader: Now, children, go in peace. Live in harmony with one another. Serve the Lord with gladness.

The grace of our Lord ✝ Jesus Christ and the love of God and the fellowship of the Holy Spirit be with you all.

Children: **Amen.**

Baa, Baa, Lost Sheep
Isaiah 53:6,7

Suggested For April 5–9, 2004

Visual Materials

- a toy sheep or lamb—stuffed or a plastic one from a child's farm set

Object Lesson

Show the toy sheep to the children. Ask: What can you tell me about sheep? Work towards responses like these: They are not very smart, they give us wool, they love to wander away and get lost, they need a shepherd to guide them. Ask: In the Bible, what does God often use as a picture of a believer? Explain that God uses a sheep or a lamb. Sometimes, God uses a sheep or a lamb as a picture of Jesus.

Make the point that in today's verses, God inspired Isaiah to write about the torture and death Jesus would one day suffer on the cross. Isaiah compared Jesus to a lamb led to the slaughter. He compares us to sheep who love to wander. Encourage the children to listen to the verse.

Bible Truth

Isaiah 53:6,7 says: **"We all, like sheep, have gone astray, each of us has turned to his own way; and the LORD has laid on him the iniquity of us all. He was oppressed and afflicted, yet he did not open his mouth; he was led like a lamb to the slaughter, and as a sheep before her shearers is silent, so he did not open his mouth."**

Isaiah uses a picture to describe a sinner. Ask: What picture does he use? Isaiah says that, because of our sin, we were like lost and wandering sheep. Ask: What danger might a lost sheep face? What danger does a sinner face? We know that a lost sheep might be killed by a wolf or some other enemy. A sinner finds himself on the dangerous road to hell. The picture of us being like these lost sheep is not a pretty one. We need a shepherd—that's where Jesus enters the scene.

Isaiah tells us that Jesus took onto himself the iniquity of us all. Ask: What is another word that might be used for *iniquity*? Jesus took our sin and placed it upon himself. He did this as he hung on the cross of Calvary. He did this because he loves us, and he did this all willingly. Jesus didn't fight to get away. He didn't try to escape from the enemies that were going to take his life. Isaiah prophesied that Jesus would go to the cross like a lamb to the slaughter. He would not even open his mouth to protest. That's exactly what Jesus did! He allowed his enemies to kill him.

We know the rest of this wonderful story. We know that Jesus did not stay a dead man in the grave. He rose on Easter Sunday to win for us salvation and to give us the sure hope of heaven. Jesus is the Shepherd, who died for the sheep who love to wander. Through his life, death, and his resurrection, he gives to his believers, his sheep, the promise of life forever in heaven.

Discussions and Applications

1. To what does Isaiah compare sinners?

2. Who is the wonderful Shepherd, who died for us?

3. What do we now know is ours because of Jesus' suffering and death?

CHAPEL TALKS FOR CHRISTIAN CHILDREN

APRIL 5–9, 2004

Leader: As children of God, we worship the Lord our Savior.

Children: Let us unite our hearts and voices to praise his holy name.

SONG OF PRAISE Christ, the Life of All the Living

Ernst C. Homburg
tr. Catherine Winkworth

Das grosse Cantional

Christ, the Life of all the liv - ing, Christ, the Death of

death, our foe, Who, thy - self for me once giv - ing

To the dark - est depths of woe— Through thy suf - f'rings,

death, and mer - it I e - ter - nal life in - her - it. Thou-sand,

thou-sand thanks shall be, Dear-est Je - sus, un - to thee.

THE MESSAGE Baa, Baa, Lost Sheep

We all, like sheep, have gone astray, each of us has turned to his own way; and the LORD has laid on him the iniquity of us all. He was oppressed and afflicted, yet he did not open his mouth; he was led like a lamb to the slaughter, and as a sheep before her shearers is silent, so he did not open his mouth (Isaiah 53:6,7).

Leader: Dear Jesus, our Shepherd, thank you for rescuing us wandering sheep. We know that our lost condition would have led us to hell. By taking upon yourself our

sins and by dying, we know that heaven is now ours. Thank you for being a Shepherd who saves. Thank you for being a Shepherd that loves the sheep. We pray this in your name, dear Savior. Amen.

HYMN Not All the Blood of Beasts

Not all the blood of beasts
On Israel's altars slain
Could give the guilty conscience peace
Or wash away the stain.

But Christ, the heav'nly Lamb,
Takes all our sins away,
A sacrifice of nobler name
And richer blood than they.

Believing, we rejoice
To see the curse remove;
We bless the Lamb with cheerful voice
And sing his bleeding love.

PSALM 79

Leader: How long, O LORD? Will you be angry forever?

Children: How long will your jealousy burn like fire?

Leader: Do not hold against us the sins of the fathers;

Children: May your mercy come quickly to meet us.

Leader: Help us, O God our Savior, for the glory of your name;

Children: Deliver us and forgive our sins for your name's sake.

Leader: Then we are your people, the sheep of your pasture, will praise you forever;

Children: From generation to generation we will recount your praise.

PRAYER REQUESTS

THE LORD'S PRAYER *(spoken together)*

OFFERINGS OF LOVE FOR JESUS

Leader: Now, children, go in peace. Live in harmony with one another. Serve the Lord with gladness.

The grace of our Lord ✝ Jesus Christ and the love of God and the fellowship of the Holy Spirit be with you all.

Children: Amen.

God Raised Jesus from the Dead
Psalm 118:15-17

Suggested for April 12–16, 2004

Visual Materials

- three medium-sized containers
- pieces of candy, rocks, dominoes, or anything that can be picked up

Object Lesson

Spread the candy (or whatever material is being used) out on a table. Choose three students. One student is allowed to use both hands. One student must place his or her right hand behind his or her back. One student must fold both hands behind his or her back. Have the assembly vote on who they think will collect the most pieces.

After you say "go," have the three students pick up as many pieces as they possibly can. The student with the most pieces in his or her container wins. Make this comment: "Life would definitely be different without our hands. Imagine what life would be like if God's 'right hand' were not working for us!"

Bible Truth

"Shouts of joy and victory resound in the tents of the righteous: 'The LORD's right hand has done mighty things! The LORD's right hand is lifted high; the LORD's right hand has done mighty things!' I will not die but live, and will proclaim what the LORD has done" (Psalm 118:15-17).

Ask: What sounds do we hear in God's Word this morning? Where are these sounds coming from? What are the people shouting? The Lord's right hand has done something so absolutely awesome that it must be said—not once— twice!

The Lord's powerful right hand has always done awesome things: the crossing of the Red Sea, the fall of Jericho, Jesus walking on water, Jesus feeding five thousand with a little boy's picnic lunch—just to name a few. All of these are little glimpses of the Lord's mighty power. But on Easter, we celebrate the most awesome act of God's right hand: The resurrection of Jesus from the dead. Jesus' resurrection proves to us that all our sins are completely forgiven, something that none of us has the power to do.

Jesus' resurrection also proves to us that we too will live even though we die. Human beings have the power to make life a little longer through medicine and surgery, but they are powerless to cure death. Jesus' powerful, living right hand will bring us from death to life with him forever.

Our Savior Jesus is living right now in heaven. We don't need to be afraid while living or dying, because Jesus will take us to heaven. This is such good news that it has a way of bubbling out of our lips: "I will not die but live, and will proclaim what the LORD has done" (Psalm 118:17).

Discussions and Applications

1. Imagine what your life would be like if Jesus' resurrection never happened.

2. Do you know any people who don't know what God's right hand has done at Easter?

3. What are some easy things you can do to share Jesus' resurrection story with them?

CHAPEL TALKS FOR CHRISTIAN CHILDREN

APRIL 12–16, 2004

Leader: As children of God, we worship the Lord our Savior.

Children: Let us unite our hearts and voices to praise his holy name.

SONG OF PRAISE *Jesus Lives**

Joan Eggert

1. Je - sus rose up from the dead On the third day, as he said.
2. "He is ris - en!" an - gels said. "Look! He is no long-er dead."
3. Je - sus lives, and so shall we. Heav'n is won for you and me!

Al - le - lu - ia! Al - le - lu - ia! Je - sus lives!
Al - le - lu - ia! Al - le - lu - ia! Je - sus lives!
Al - le - lu - ia! Al - le - lu - ia! Je - sus lives!

THE MESSAGE God Raised Jesus from the Dead

Shouts of joy and victory resound in the tents of the righteous: "The LORD's right hand has done mighty things! The LORD's right hand is lifted high; the LORD's right hand has done mighty things!" I will not die but live, and will proclaim what the LORD has done (Psalm 118:15-17).

Leader: Lord Jesus Christ, we are weak and sinful. You are strong and holy. By the great power of your strength, you defeated death for us. By your perfect life, innocent death, and glorious resurrection, you took away our sins. Until we shout your praises with the angels in heaven, we will continue to proclaim your good news here on earth. Help us do this for Jesus' sake. Amen.

HYMN Christ the Lord Is Risen Today

"Christ the Lord is ris'n today!"
Saints on earth and angels say;
Raise your joys and triumphs high;
Sing, O heav'ns, and earth, reply.

Love's redeeming work is done,
Fought the fight, the battle won;
Lo, our sun's eclipse is o'er,
Lo, he sets in blood no more.

Vain the stone, the watch, the seal;
Christ has burst the gates of hell.
Death in vain forbids his rise;
Christ has opened paradise.

PSALM 118

Leader: The LORD is my strength and my song;

Children: He has become my salvation.

Leader: "The LORD's right hand is lifted high;

Children: The LORD's right hand has done mighty things!"

Leader: I will not die but live,

Children: And will proclaim what the LORD has done.

PRAYER REQUESTS

THE LORD'S PRAYER *(spoken together)*

OFFERINGS OF LOVE FOR JESUS

Leader: Now, children, go in peace. Live in harmony with one another. Serve the Lord with gladness.

The grace of our Lord ✝ Jesus Christ and the love of God and the fellowship of the Holy Spirit be with you all.

Children: Amen.

Jesus Is the Cornerstone
Psalm 118:22-24

35

Suggested for April 19–23, 2004

Visual Materials

- a deck of cards
- some wood blocks
- a brick or rock

Object Lesson

Make an effort or two to build a house of cards. The students will soon see that a house of cards easily falls. Second, make a small structure of wood blocks and push it over. Finally, show the students the brick or the rock. Ask the students what a building would be like if it was built entirely out of this material. Point out that a brick house is a good, dependable house.

Explain that the most important brick of a building is called the cornerstone. It is the brick that all the other bricks rest upon. Jesus is called a capstone, or a cornerstone. He's the only brick worth building a life upon.

Bible Truth

"The stone the builders rejected has become the capstone; the LORD has done this, and it is marvelous in our eyes. This is the day the LORD has made; let us rejoice and be glad in it" (Psalm 118:22-24).

Our selection from Psalm 118 was written hundreds of years before the time of Jesus. It is a marvelous prophecy of the suffering and glory of our Savior.

The Son of God—the "capstone"—was rejected by the people who were supposed to believe in him. Jesus himself quotes Psalm 118:22 in Matthew 21:42: "Jesus said to them, 'Have you never read in the Scriptures: "The stone the builders rejected has become the capstone"?'" Immediately after Jesus spoke those words, we hear a group of builders rejecting the saving stone: "When the chief priests and the Pharisees heard Jesus' parables, they knew he was talking about them. They looked for a way to arrest him" (Matt. 21:45,46). The stone's rejection was finalized with the cries of "Crucify him!" and "Release Barabbas!" (Luke 23:18,20).

Notice the "marvelous" thing that God did. God took the stone that the builders had thrown away—hated, rejected, crucified, killed, and buried—and made that very stone the most important stone in the building. Jesus now lives again. As the living, powerful Lord, Jesus is the stone that his church is built upon.

Those who build their lives on the solid rock of Jesus Christ will live forever. Those who continue to reject Jesus the rock will be crushed under God's judgment.

Rejoice and be glad that the Lord has built you safely upon the cornerstone, his Son, Jesus. Rejoice because the devil cannot knock down what God has built upon his Son!

Discussions and Applications

1. Where does your family go when there is a bad storm? Why do they go there?

2. What are ways we can build our lives upon Jesus our rock?

3. What are some ways that people throw away, or reject, the stone called Jesus Christ?

CHAPEL TALKS FOR CHRISTIAN CHILDREN
APRIL 19–23, 2004

Leader: As children of God, we worship the Lord our Savior.

Children: Let us unite our hearts and voices to praise his holy name.

SONG OF PRAISE *Jesus Lives**

Joan Eggert

1. Je - sus rose up from the dead On the third day, as he said.
2. "He is ris - en!" an - gels said. "Look! He is no long-er dead."
3. Je - sus lives, and so shall we. Heav'n is won for you and me!

Al - le - lu - ia! Al - le - lu - ia! Je - sus lives!
Al - le - lu - ia! Al - le - lu - ia! Je - sus lives!
Al - le - lu - ia! Al - le - lu - ia! Je - sus lives!

THE MESSAGE Jesus Is the Cornerstone

The stone the builders rejected has become the capstone; the LORD *has done this, and it is marvelous in our eyes. This is the day the* LORD *has made; let us rejoice and be glad in it* (Psalm 118:22-24).

Leader: Lord Jesus, you are the rock of our salvation. Forgive us for the times when we have been tempted to build our lives on foundations other than you. Help us build our lives always upon you. Give us ears to listen to your Word, hearts that are filled with faith, and lips that are eager to praise you. Help us to always appreciate the marvelous thing you did for us when you suffered, died, and rose again so that we can be with you forever! Amen.

HYMN God Loved the World So That He Gave

God loved the world so that he gave
His only Son the lost to save
That all who would in him believe
Should everlasting life receive.

Christ is the solid rock of faith,
Who was made flesh and suffered death.
All who confide in him alone
Are built on this chief cornerstone.

God would not have the sinner die—
His Son with saving grace is nigh.
His Spirit in the Word does teach
How we the blessed goal may reach.

PSALM 118

Leader: The stone the builders rejected

Children: Has become the capstone;

Leader: The LORD has done this,

Children: And it is marvelous in our eyes.

Leader: This is the day the LORD has made;

Children: Let us rejoice and be glad in it.

PRAYER REQUESTS

THE LORD'S PRAYER *(spoken together)*

OFFERINGS OF LOVE FOR JESUS

Leader: Now, children, go in peace. Live in harmony with one another. Serve the Lord with gladness. The grace of our Lord ✠ Jesus Christ and the love of God and the fellowship of the Holy Spirit be with you all.

Children: Amen.

Jesus Cares for Us
Psalm 23:1-3

36

Suggested for April 26–30, 2004

Visual Materials

- basic medical supplies (Band-aids, aspirin, antiseptic, etc.)

Object Lesson

Demonstrate briefly what can be done with each of the medical supplies that you exhibit. Ask: What would life be like without these basic medical supplies? Mention that doctors, nurses, and EMTs are people that have dedicated their lives to caring for people who need medical help.

Explain that in Bible times we often hear about shepherds. Shepherds are people who care for sheep. Sheep can get lost easily. They are easy prey for predators—lions, bears, and wolves. They are easily injured in rough country. Jesus calls himself the Good Shepherd. We will see how the Good Shepherd takes care of you and me—his sheep—still today.

Bible Truth

"The LORD is my shepherd, I shall not be in want. He makes me lie down in green pastures, he leads me beside quiet waters, he restores my soul. He guides me in paths of righteousness for his name's sake" (Psalm 23:1-3).

Shepherds do their best to take care of their sheep. But even the best shepherds make mistakes. They can doze off. Wolves can sneak in and scatter their flocks. Favorite waterholes can dry up. Tender little lambs can die in spite of a shepherd's best efforts. So it is with sinful people: their best efforts are not good enough.

The good news for us is that our salvation and security do not depend on human shepherds. God himself is our Shepherd. And Jesus, the Good Shepherd, knows how to take excellent care of his sheep. He knows our real needs. He knows how to take care of those needs.

Life can be tiring. We sin. We repent of that sin. And in spite of our best efforts, we often fall into the same sins again. This wears down our hearts and burdens our consciences. Our Shepherd provides us with rest. Our Shepherd provides us with nourishing food and water. The Good Shepherd makes our souls strong. How? Through the peace of his forgiveness! The burden of sin is removed. Forgiveness and peace take its place.

Our Shepherd provides us with guidance. Life has all sorts of paths that we can follow. All but one of those paths lead us away from God. People think they can reach heaven by the good things that they do. Other people do not even believe in Jesus or in heaven. Those paths lead to eternal life in hell! Our Good Shepherd leads us on the path that leads straight to heaven. Jesus' Word helps us stay on the path that will finally bring us to him.

Discussions and Applications

1. Do your remember how you felt when you were lost in a store or mall and then found? How happy we are that Jesus has found us!

2. What are some ways that our Good Shepherd leads us to "green pastures" and "quiet waters"?

CHAPEL TALKS FOR CHRISTIAN CHILDREN

APRIL 26–30, 2004

Leader: As children of God, we worship the Lord our Savior.

Children: **Let us unite our hearts and voices to praise his holy name.**

SONG OF PRAISE *Jesus Lives**

Joan Eggert

1. Je - sus rose up from the dead On the third day, as he said.
2. "He is ris - en!" an - gels said. "Look! He is no long-er dead."
3. Je - sus lives, and so shall we. Heav'n is won for you and me!

Al - le - lu - ia! Al - le - lu - ia! Al - le - lu - ia! Je - sus lives!
Al - le - lu - ia! Al - le - lu - ia! Al - le - lu - ia! Je - sus lives!
Al - le - lu - ia! Al - le - lu - ia! Al - le - lu - ia! Je - sus lives!

THE MESSAGE *Jesus Cares for Us*

The LORD is my shepherd, I shall not be in want. He makes me lie down in green pastures, he leads me beside quiet waters, he restores my soul. He guides me in paths of righteousness for his name's sake (Psalm 23:1-3).

Leader: Lord Jesus, you are our Good Shepherd. We thank you for all the tender, loving care that you give to us. Without you, we would be lost! But you found us. You give us your Word to feed our souls and keep us on the path that leads to the pastures of heaven. Help us listen to your voice in your Word for guidance every day of our lives. Amen.

HYMN The Lord's My Shepherd; I'll Not Want

The Lord's my shepherd; I'll not want.
He makes me down to lie
In pastures green; he leadeth me
The quiet waters by.

My soul he doth restore again
And me to walk doth make
Within the paths of righteousness,
E'en for his own name's sake.

PSALM 23

Leader: The LORD is my shepherd,

Children: **I shall not be in want.**

Leader: He makes me lie down in green pastures,

Children: **He leads me beside quiet waters,**

Leader: He restores my soul.

Children: **He guides me in paths of righteousness for his name's sake.**

PRAYER REQUESTS

THE LORD'S PRAYER *(spoken together")*

OFFERINGS OF LOVE FOR JESUS

Leader: Now, children, go in peace. Live in harmony with one another. Serve the Lord with gladness.

The grace of our Lord ✝ Jesus Christ and the love of God and the fellowship of the Holy Spirit be with you all.

Children: **Amen.**

We Don't Have to Be Afraid
Psalm 23:4

37

Suggested for May 3–7, 2004

Visual Materials

- a pair of sunglasses and some suntan lotion
- a flashlight and a candle

Object Lesson

Show the students the sunglasses and the suntan lotion. Ask them when they might use these items (at a beach, while fishing, at a park, and so on).

Now show the flashlight and the candle to the students. Ask them when they might have to use these items (in dark woods while camping, when power goes out in the middle of the night, and so on). Point out that we don't like being in the dark. We do what we can to make some light. When we have a light in the darkness, we feel safe.

Explain that today God wants to talk to the group about the dark—the darkness of death. Death can be scary. But with Jesus as our Good Shepherd, we don't need to be afraid of the dark.

Bible Truth

"Even though I walk through the valley of the shadow of death, I will fear no evil, for you are with me; your rod and your staff, they comfort me" (Psalm 23:4).

(Dr. Brug in his People's Bible commentary on Psalms states, "The 'valley of the shadow of death' may also be translated 'the darkest valley,'" p. 113.) There are many dangers in Christians' lives that are potentially scary. Friends hurt our feelings. Moms and dads do not always get along. Family members get sick and even die. Even though we think we are going to live a long time, we too will die one day. All of these situations seem dark and scary.

But Jesus is always there to protect his sheep. In John 10:11 Jesus says: "I am the good shepherd. The good shepherd lays down his life for the sheep." Jesus loves us so much that he walked "though the valley of the shadow of death" for us by dying on the cross. If Jesus loves us that much, he will not let the scary problems of life take us away from him.

The devil is real. Our problems are real. The dark things that scare us are real. But the good news for today is that Jesus is real too. He died and rose again. When he did, he defeated the devil. Our problems have been beaten too. Jesus has forgiven our sins. Jesus lives! He has promised that he will be with us always—to the very end of the age. That takes the fear out of his sheep and replaces it with the comfort of his salvation.

Discussions and Applications

1. What are some of the different ways that God keeps our bodies safe?

2. Who are the different people Jesus uses to keep our souls safe?

CHAPEL TALKS FOR CHRISTIAN CHILDREN

MAY 3–7, 2004

Leader: As children of God, we worship the Lord our Savior.

Children: **Let us unite our hearts and voices to praise his holy name.**

SONG OF PRAISE *Jesus Lives**

Joan Eggert

1. Je - sus rose up from the dead On the third day, as he said.
2. "He is ris - en!" an - gels said. "Look! He is no long-er dead."
3. Je - sus lives, and so shall we. Heav'n is won for you and me!

Al - le - lu - ia! Al - le - lu - ia! Al - le - lu - ia! Je - sus lives!
Al - le - lu - ia! Al - le - lu - ia! Al - le - lu - ia! Je - sus lives!
Al - le - lu - ia! Al - le - lu - ia! Al - le - lu - ia! Je - sus lives!

THE MESSAGE We Don't Have to Be Afraid

Even though I walk through the valley of the shadow of death,
I will fear no evil, for you are with me; your rod and your staff,
they comfort me (Psalm 23:4).

Leader: The King of love my shepherd is,
Whose goodness fails me never;
I nothing lack if I am his,
And he is mine forever.

In death's dark vale I fear no ill
With you, dear Lord, beside me;
Your rod and staff my comfort still,
Your cross before to guide me. Amen.

HYMN I Am Jesus' Little Lamb

I am Jesus' little lamb;
Ever glad at heart I am,
For my shepherd gently guides me,
Knows my needs and well provides me,
Loves me ev'ry day the same,
Even calls me by my name.

Day by day, at home, away,
Jesus is my staff and stay.
When I hunger, Jesus feeds me,
Into pleasant pastures leads me;
When I thirst, he bids me go
Where the quiet waters flow.

Who so happy as I am,
Even now the shepherd's lamb?
And when my short life is ended,
By his angel hosts attended,
He shall fold me to his breast,
There within his arms to rest.

PSALM 23

Leader: The LORD is my shepherd,

Children: **I shall not be in want.**

Leader: Even though I walk through the valley of the shadow of death,

Children: **I will fear no evil, for you are with me;**

Leader: Your rod and your staff,

Children: **They comfort me.**

PRAYER REQUESTS

THE LORD'S PRAYER *(spoken together)*

OFFERINGS OF LOVE FOR JESUS

Leader: Now, children, go in peace. Live in harmony with one another. Serve the Lord with gladness.
The grace of our Lord ✝ Jesus Christ and the love of God and the fellowship of the Holy Spirit be with you all.

Children: **Amen.**

God Blesses Us
Psalm 23:5,6

Suggested for May 10–14, 2004

Visual Materials

- two or three invitations to a picnic
- a "picnic" lunch of yesterday's leftovers (half-eaten apple, stale chips, and so on—the older the better) placed in a brown bag or picnic basket

Object Lesson

Take one of your invitations and read it to the students. Next, give invitations to two or three students. Have them come to the front of the assembly where you will unpack your "picnic."

Make a big point of what you have packed. Ask the students how they would feel if they got all dressed up to attend a banquet of leftovers (offended, angry, and so on). Point out that if we as human beings try to serve our best meals when we invite people over for supper, how much more God prepares the greatest of banquets for his people to eat!

Bible Truth

"You prepare a table before me in the presence of my enemies. You anoint my head with oil; my cup overflows. Surely goodness and love will follow me all the days of my life, and I will dwell in the house of the LORD forever" (Psalm 23:5,6).

For the previous two weeks, we have heard about our Good Shepherd and his sheep. Now the picture of the Shepherd changes slightly to a Shepherd-King. At the time of David, kings were often called shepherds of their people.

In ancient times, kings would throw large banquets with the best food. Dining at the king's table was a great honor. (Dr. Brug in the People's Bible commentary notes, "[The king's] guests were anointed with oil as a symbol of the honor and joy of being in the royal court" p. 114.) Food was not in short supply, neither was the best of wines.

If worldly kings treated their guests that way, how much better the banquet is that God prepares for us! He offers us a wonderful banquet of the best spiritual food and drink. Our Shepherd-King pours his precious oil on our heads to show us we are his honored guests. Our cups overflow with the goodness of our God. The best news is that our Shepherd-King's banquet will never end! We will dwell in God's house forever.

But don't only think of heaven! Right now God gives us a special meal of his forgiveness. It's called the Lord's Supper. Jesus said that he wants to give us his body and blood with the bread and wine for our forgiveness. Right now we might not feel real oil being poured on our heads, but we have had water poured on our heads in the name of Father, Son, and Holy Spirit. In Baptism, God forgave us our sins and sat us down at his banquet table with the rest of our family in Christ.

Discussions and Application:

1. Let's pretend that someone came into school and stole all of our lunches while we were out for recess. How would we feel?

2. How will our souls feel if they are not fed for a long time?

3. What are ways our soul can be well fed?

CHAPEL TALKS FOR CHRISTIAN CHILDREN

MAY 10–14, 2004

Leader: As children of God, we worship the Lord our Savior.

Children: **Let us unite our hearts and voices to praise his holy name.**

SONG OF PRAISE *Jesus Lives**

Joan Eggert

1. Je - sus rose up from the dead On the third day, as he said.
2. "He is ris - en!" an - gels said. "Look! He is no long - er dead."
3. Je - sus lives, and so shall we. Heav'n is won for you and me!

Al-le-lu - ia! Al-le-lu - ia! Al-le-lu - ia! Je - sus lives!
Al-le-lu - ia! Al-le-lu - ia! Al-le-lu - ia! Je - sus lives!
Al-le-lu - ia! Al-le-lu - ia! Al-le-lu - ia! Je - sus lives!

THE MESSAGE God Blesses Us

You prepare a table before me in the presence of my enemies. You anoint my head with oil; my cup overflows. Surely goodness and love will follow me all the days of my life, and I will dwell in the house of the LORD forever (Psalm 23:5,6).

Leader: Lord Jesus, you are our Good Shepherd. You are our King. We thank you for all of your wonderful gifts. You have given us clothing and shoes, food and drink, and all that we need to keep our bodies and lives. You have also given us a wonderful banquet of spiritual foods that will keep our souls alive and faithful to you. Be with us dear Jesus until we can eat this wonderful banquet with you face-to-face in heaven. Amen.

HYMN The Lord's My Shepherd; I'll Not Want

The Lord's my shepherd; I'll not want.
He makes me down to lie
In pastures green; he leadeth me
The quiet waters by.

My table thou hast furnished
In presence of my foes;
My head thou dost with oil anoint,
And my cup overflows.

Goodness and mercy, all my life,
Shall surely follow me,
And in God's house forevermore
My dwelling-place shall be.

PSALM 23

Leader: The LORD is my shepherd,

Children: **I shall not be in want.**

Leader: You prepare a table before me

Children: **In the presence of my enemies.**

Leader: You anoint my head with oil;

Children: **My cup overflows.**

Leader: Surely goodness and love will follow me all the days of my life,

Children: **And I will dwell in the house of the LORD forever.**

PRAYER REQUESTS

THE LORD'S PRAYER *(spoken together)*

OFFERINGS OF LOVE FOR JESUS

Leader: Now, children, go in peace. Live in harmony with one another. Serve the Lord with gladness.

The grace of our Lord ✝ Jesus Christ and the love of God and the fellowship of the Holy Spirit be with you all.

Children: **Amen.**

Showing Joy in the Lord
Psalm 47:1-4

Suggested for May 17–21, 2004

Visual Materials

- a pair of big mittens

Object Lesson

Have an older student come forward. Ask the student to clap four beats four times. Next, have the student clap as quickly and loudly as possible. Now have that student put the mittens on. Ask the student to clap quickly and loudly again.

Ask the students what the difference is between the two sounds. Note that the bright sounds of clapping get us moving on a basketball court, show we love a piece of music at a concert, and encourage one another at a track meet. The dull thud of mittens is not exciting. Make the point that we want to join in with the bright claps of Psalm 47 in praise to our God. When it comes to praising God, we never want to have mittens on!

Bible Truth

"Clap your hands, all you nations; shout to God with cries of joy. How awesome is the LORD Most High, the great King over all the earth! He subdued nations under us, peoples under our feet. He chose our inheritance for us, the pride of Jacob, whom he loved" (Psalm 47:1-4).

Think of some of the loudest sounds we have ever heard people make: 20,000 people cheering for a home run at a baseball stadium, 50,000 cheering voices and 100,000 clapping hands at a Super Bowl, thousands upon thousands of people singing and clapping at a concert. These are all loud sounds. Each one of these sounds falls far short of the thunderous clapping that rises up to heaven in praise to our Lord. The psalmist invites all nations to join in clapping and shouting of God's praises. Professional baseball might be a big deal. A Super Bowl might be stupendous. But these count for absolutely nothing compared to the awesome greatness of our Lord the King!

Why does God deserve the praise of all people? Because he is powerful? Because he created people to praise him? All of that is true, but God deserves the praises of all people because he is the King who keeps his promises! God promised the Israelites that they would enter and conquer the Promised Land. God kept his promise.

God gave the Israelites the Promised Land so that you and I could someday enter into God's eternal promised land of heaven. Remember what happened in the Promised Land? Micah prophesied that a Savior was to be born in Bethlehem Ephrathah (Micah 5:2). Isaiah prophesied that this Savior would suffer the sin and iniquity of his people (Isaiah 53). David prophesied that this Savior would rise again from the dead (Psalm 16:9-11). God kept every one of his promises made in the Promised Land so all who believe in Jesus would go to heaven.

All the people of the earth—whether you come from America or Afghanistan—have something to clap, sing, and shout about!

Discussions and Applications

1. What would it be like to not be able to clap at a basketball or football game?

2. What would life be like if you could not praise God?

3. What is the one promise that the Lord is still waiting to keep?

CHAPEL TALKS FOR CHRISTIAN CHILDREN

MAY 17–21, 2004

Leader: As children of God, we worship the Lord our Savior.

Children: Let us unite our hearts and voices to praise his holy name.

SONG OF PRAISE Alleluia! Sing to Jesus

William C. Dix

Ludwig van Beethoven

1. Al - le - lu - ia! Sing to Je - sus; His the scep - ter,
2. Al - le - lu - ia! Not as or - phans Are we left in

his the throne; Al - le - lu - ia! His the tri - umph,
sor - row now; Al - le - lu - ia! He is near us;

His the vic - to - ry a - lone. Hark! The songs of
Faith be - lieves, nor ques - tions how. Though the cloud from

peace - ful Zi - on Thun - der - like a might - y flood:
sight re - ceived him When the for - ty days were o'er, "Je - sus
Shall our

out of ev - 'ry na - tion Has re - deemed us by his blood."
hearts for - get his prom - ise: "I am with you ev - er - more"?

Leader: Lord God, heavenly Father, you have given us so much to clap and shout about! You gave us your Son, Jesus. You brought us into your family. And one day in the future, you will bring us to our promised land of heaven. Send us your Holy Spirit, that we may continue to believe each of your promises in your Word. In Jesus' name we pray. Amen.

HYMN God of Mercy, God of Grace

God of mercy, God of grace,
Show the brightness of your face.
Shine upon us, Savior, shine;
Fill your Church with light divine,
And your saving health extend
To the earth's remotest end.

Let the people praise you, Lord!
Be by all that live adored.
Let the nations shout and sing
Glory to their Savior King,
At your feet their tribute pay,
And your holy will obey.

PSALM 47

Leader: Clap your hands, all you nations;
Children: Shout to God with cries of joy.

Leader: How awesome is the LORD Most High,
Children: The great King over all the earth!

Leader: He subdued nations under us,
Children: Peoples under our feet.

Leader: He chose our inheritance for us,
Children: The pride of Jacob, whom he loved.

PRAYER REQUESTS

THE LORD'S PRAYER (spoken together)

OFFERINGS OF LOVE FOR JESUS

Leader: Now, children, go in peace. Live in harmony with one another. Serve the Lord with gladness.

The grace of our Lord ✝ Jesus Christ and the love of God and the fellowship of the Holy Spirit be with you all.

Children: Amen.

THE MESSAGE Showing Joy in the Lord

Clap your hands, all you nations; shout to God with cries of joy. How awesome is the LORD Most High, the great King over all the earth! He subdued nations under us, peoples under our feet. He chose our inheritance for us, the pride of Jacob, whom he loved (Psalm 47:1-4).

Jesus Ascended Amid Joy
Psalm 47:5,6

Suggested for May 24–28, 2004

Visual Materials

- a pillow
- a large megaphone made out of poster board (other options: electric megaphone or church microphone turned up rather loud)

Object Lesson

Place the pillow in front of you. Let the students know that you have something very important to tell them. Bury your face in the pillow and shout these words: "God has ascended amid shouts of joy!" See how many of the students understood you. Now take your megaphone. Loudly and clearly speak these words: "God has ascended amid shouts of joy, the LORD amid the sounding of trumpets!" Ask the students who understood you this time.

Note that today the children will hear the saints and angels shouting and singing the praises of God in heaven. They, in turn, will want to be a big megaphone in God's hands—shouting his praises for all to hear on earth!

Bible Truth

"God has ascended amid shouts of joy, the LORD amid the sounding of trumpets. Sing praises to God, sing praises; sing praises to our King, sing praises" (Psalm 47:5,6).

The picture behind these verses is of a king who has returned from a battle victorious. He has won. His enemies lost. The people shout with joy. The trumpets blare. Even today we have victory parades something like this. We march people down the streets of New York, throwing tons of paper into the air while people shout and cheer.

Psalm 47 speaks of God's ascension to his position of glory, honor, and praise in heaven. But the very fact that we see God ascending amid shouts of joy tells us something very important. If God ascends in victory to heaven, that tells us that he had to descend to earth to fight a battle.

Whom did he fight against? Sin, death, and the power of the devil. Sin has been paid for. Death is defeated through the resurrection of Jesus on Easter. The power of the devil has been broken through Jesus' death and resurrection. As a matter of fact, the Bible clearly tells us that the devil lost his battle with God: "There was war in heaven. Michael and his angels fought against the dragon, and the dragon and his angels fought back. But he was not strong enough, and they lost their place in heaven" (Revelation 12:7,8).

Jesus' ascension amid the shouts and praises of the saints and angels proves to us that his victory over sin is complete. It shows us that Jesus, not the devil, rules heaven and earth for our good. It reminds us that just as Jesus ascended into heaven, so one day soon he will come back and take us to be with him in heaven. Until then, spend your days shouting and singing your Savior's praises. Be a megaphone of God's good news in the world.

Discussions and Applications

1. What would your life be like right now if Jesus never ascended into heaven?
2. What is a way that you can "shout for God" in the world?

CHAPEL TALKS FOR CHRISTIAN CHILDREN

MAY 24-28, 2004

Leader: As children of God, we worship the Lord our Savior.

Children: Let us unite our hearts and voices to praise his holy name.

SONG OF PRAISE Alleluia! Sing to Jesus

William C. Dix   Ludwig van Beethoven

1. Al - le - lu - ia!   Sing to Je - sus;   His the scep - ter,
2. Al - le - lu - ia!   Not as or - phans   Are we left in

his the throne;   Al - le - lu - ia!   His the tri - umph,
sor - row now;   Al - le - lu - ia!   He is near us;

His the vic - to - ry a - lone.   Hark! The songs of
Faith be - lieves, nor ques - tions how.   Though the cloud from

peace-ful Zi - on Thun - der-like a might-y flood: "Je - sus
sight re-ceived him When the for - ty days were o'er,   Shall our

out of ev - 'ry na - tion Has re-deemed us by his blood."   "Je - sus
hearts for - get his prom-ise: "I am with you ev - er - more"?

THE MESSAGE Jesus Ascended Amid Joy

God has ascended amid shouts of joy, the LORD amid the sounding of trumpets. Sing praises to God, sing praises; sing praises to our King, sing praises (Psalm 47:5,6).

Leader: Lord Jesus Christ, we praise you that you ascended into heaven. Your Word tells us that you have gone there to prepare a place for us. Because of your forgiveness, we look forward to being with you in heaven forever. Until we see you face-to-face in heaven, use us to shout and sing your praises in this life. We ask this in Jesus' name. Amen.

HYMN Hail the Day That Sees Him Rise

**Hail the day that sees him rise
To his throne above the skies!
Christ, the Lamb for sinners giv'n,
Reascends his native heav'n.**

There the glorious triumph waits:
Lift your heads, eternal gates.
He has conquered death and sin;
Take the King of glory in!

See, the heav'n its Lord receives,
Yet he loves the earth he leaves;
Though returning to his throne,
Still he calls mankind his own.

PSALM 47

Leader: Clap your hands, all you nations;

Children: Shout to God with cries of joy.

Leader: God has ascended amid shouts of joy,

Children: The LORD amid the sounding of trumpets.

Leader: Sing praises to God, sing praises;

Children: Sing praises to our King, sing praises.

PRAYER REQUESTS

THE LORD'S PRAYER (*spoken together*)

OFFERINGS OF LOVE FOR JESUS

Leader: Now, children, go in peace. Live in harmony with one another. Serve the Lord with gladness.

The grace of our Lord ✝ Jesus Christ and the love of God and the fellowship of the Holy Spirit be with you all.

Children: Amen.

Jesus Reigns Over All
Psalm 47:7-9

Suggested for the May 31–June 4, 2004

Visual Materials

- a folding chair, a stool, a pastor's chair from the front of the church (different chairs of any type will do)

Object Lesson

Explain to the students that you have several different types of chairs. Each of these chairs serves a different purpose. A folding chair is used for potlucks. A stool is a handy seat that can be easily stored away. A pastor's chair is a formal chair where the pastor sits when he is leading the people of God in worship.

Ask the students if they can name some other types of chairs and what those chairs are used for (recliner, lawn chair, bleacher seat, and so on).

Point out that the ultimate chair is a throne. Ask: What is the use of the throne? Today the group will see how God rules heaven and earth from his great throne.

Bible Truth

"God is the King of all the earth; sing to him a psalm of praise. God reigns over the nations; God is seated on his holy throne. The nobles of the nations assemble as the people of the God of Abraham, for the kings of the earth belong to God; he is greatly exalted" (Psalm 47:7-9).

Kings sit on thrones. Our God sits on his throne. The throne is symbolic of our Lord's kingship. Earthly kings rule over individual nations. Some are large. Some are small. The Roman Empire at the time of Jesus was huge. The British Empire of one hundred years ago was the largest empire the world has ever seen. No man-made empire has ever ruled the entire earth.

But there is a God-made empire that rules over the entire earth. God is King of all the earth. People from every nation belong to his family. One by one God's kingdom grows, one heart at a time. Jesus told us that the kingdom of God is within us. Think of that, the King of "all the earth" rules and lives in our hearts!

From his holy throne God rules all things for the good of his people—the church. Jesus loves us so much that he was willing to die for us. If he loves us that much, he certainly won't leave us alone here on earth.

Jesus, as King of heaven and earth, deserves our songs of praise. Our Bible text tells us to sing a psalm of praise to God. A big part of worship is praising God because he is God and we are his people. In our worship we thank him for his forgiveness, his rule in our hearts, his rule of our world, and his glory in heaven.

Discussions and Applications

1. What would life be like if there were no government (no police, no fire department, no judges, and so on)?

2. What would life be like if God were not ruling heaven and earth?

3. Long ago, the wise men brought gifts to baby King Jesus. What are some gifts that we can bring to Jesus, the great King of heaven and earth?

CHAPEL TALKS FOR CHRISTIAN CHILDREN

MAY 31–JUNE 4, 2004

Leader: As children of God, we worship the Lord our Savior.

Children: Let us unite our hearts and voices to praise his holy name.

SONG OF PRAISE Alleluia! Sing to Jesus

William C. Dix

Ludwig van Beethoven

1. Al - le - lu - ia! Sing to Je - sus; His the scep - ter,
2. Al - le - lu - ia! Not as or - phans Are we left in

his the throne; Al - le - lu - ia! His the tri - umph,
sor - row now; Al - le - lu - ia! He is near us;

His the vic - to - ry a - lone. Hark! The songs of
Faith be - lieves, nor ques - tions how. Though the cloud from

peace - ful. Zi - on Thun - der - like a might - y flood; "Je - sus
sight re - ceived him When the - for - ty days were o'er, Shall our

out of ev - 'ry na - tion Has re - deemed us by his blood."
hearts for - get his prom - ise: "I am with you ev - er - more"?

THE MESSAGE Jesus Reigns Over All

*God is the King of all the earth; sing to him a psalm of praise.
God reigns over the nations; God is seated on his holy throne.
The nobles of the nations assemble as the people of the God of
Abraham, for the kings of the earth belong to God; he is greatly
exalted (Psalm 47:7-9).*

Leader: Dear Jesus, you are the King of heaven and earth. Your ascension into heaven proves that you rule over heaven and earth. Bless the work of your churches and schools, that many more people might become members of your kingdom through faith. In Jesus' name we pray. Amen.

HYMN Crown Him with Many Crowns

Crown him with many crowns,
The Lamb upon his throne;
Hark how the heav'nly anthem drowns
All music but its own.
Awake, my soul, and sing
Of him who died for thee,
And hail him as thy matchless King
Through all eternity.

Crown him the Lord of heav'n,
Enthroned in worlds above;
Crown him the King to whom is giv'n
The wondrous name of Love.
Crown him with many crowns
As thrones before him fall;
Crown him, ye kings, with many crowns
For he is King of all.

PSALM 47

Leader: God is the King of all the earth;

Children: Sing to him a psalm of praise.

Leader: God reigns over the nations;

Children: God is seated on his holy throne.

Leader: The kings of the earth belong to God;

Children: He is greatly exalted.

PRAYER REQUESTS

THE LORD'S PRAYER (*spoken together*)

OFFERINGS OF LOVE FOR JESUS

Leader: Now, children, go in peace. Live in harmony with one another. Serve the Lord with gladness.

The grace of our Lord ✠ Jesus Christ and the love of God and the fellowship of the Holy Spirit be with you all.

Children: Amen.

Jesus Is the Lamb of God
Revelation 5:12,13

Suggested for June 7–11, 2004

Visual Materials

- church artwork, banners, or pastoral stoles with the symbol of Christ the Lamb on them

Object Lesson

Encourage the students to look around the sanctuary. Ask what symbols they see (a cross, Trinity symbols, and so on). Discuss briefly what each of these means.

Explain that one of the greatest symbols of our Christian faith is the lamb. When we think of lambs, we think of fuzzy, little animals on the green hills outside of town. Point out that today the group will look at the Bible picture of Jesus as God's Lamb.

Bible Truth

"In a loud voice they sang: 'Worthy is the Lamb, who was slain, to receive power and wealth and wisdom and strength and honor and glory and praise!' Then I heard every creature in heaven and on earth and under the earth and on the sea, and all that is in them, singing: 'To him who sits on the throne and to the Lamb be praise and honor and glory and power, for ever and ever!'" (Revelation 5:12,13).

When the Bible speaks of lambs, it often connects them with sacrifice. Lamb and offering go together roughly 40 times in the NIV Bible. Every morning and evening a lamb was burned in the temple. Sin and guilt offerings featured the offering of a lamb. The Passover featured a lamb without blemish or defect as the main course.

Jesus is "the Lamb, who was slain." Why was this lamb slain? Just ask John the Baptist. Jesus is the "Lamb of God, who takes away the sin of the world!" (John 1:29). The Lamb's sacrifice was so awesome, so total, so complete, and so precious that another little lamb would never have to lose its life! Jesus' sacrifice of himself is a sacrifice made once for all. The author of Hebrews says it this way: "Unlike the other high priests, he does not need to offer sacrifices day after day, first for his own sins, and then for the sins of the people. He sacrificed for their sins once for all when he offered himself" (Hebrews 7:27). The Lamb has taken our sin away. No further sacrifice is needed.

A sacrifice this great deserves recognition! And Jesus receives that recognition from all the saints and angels alike. Jesus is worthy of that heavenly praise. When we worship Jesus, we are showing him that he is worthy of our praise too. Practice praising your Savior your whole life long. Why? Because one thing we can count on in heaven is singing the Lamb's praises!

Discussions and Applications

1. What are some excuses people make for not worshiping the Lamb?

2. Our worship of the Lamb will not end in heaven. What does this say to us about our worship of the Lamb during the summer months?

CHAPEL TALKS FOR CHRISTIAN CHILDREN

JUNE 7–11, 2004

Leader: As children of God, we worship the Lord our Savior.

Children: **Let us unite our hearts and voices to praise his holy name.**

SONG OF PRAISE Alleluia! Sing to Jesus

William C. Dix   Ludwig van Beethoven

1. Al - le - lu - ia! Sing to Je - sus; His the scep - ter,
2. Al - le - lu - ia! Not as or - phans Are we left in

his the throne; Al - le - lu - ia! His the tri - umph,
sor - row now; Al - le - lu - ia! He is near us;

His the vic - to - ry a - lone. Hark! The songs of
Faith be - lieves, nor ques - tions how. Though the cloud from

peace - ful Zi - on Thun - der - like a might - y flood:
sight re - ceived him When the - for - ty days were o'er,
"Je - sus
Shall our

out of ev - 'ry na - tion Has re - deemed us by his blood."
hearts for - get his prom - ise: "I am with you ev - er - more"?

THE MESSAGE Jesus Is the Lamb of God

In a loud voice they sang: "Worthy is the Lamb, who was slain, to receive power and wealth and wisdom and strength and honor and glory and praise!" Then I heard every creature in heaven and on earth and under the earth and on the sea, and all that is in them, singing: "To him who sits on the throne and

to the Lamb be praise and honor and glory and power, for ever and ever!" (Revelation 5:12,13).

Leader: Lamb of God, you have taken away the sin of the world. You have shown us your mercy and peace through the forgiveness of our sins. You sacrificed yourself for our forgiveness. Now you live again forever and ever. Help us to always treasure your sacrifice for us. Help us always to give you the praise and honor you deserve. To you be the glory now and forever! Amen.

HYMN Come, Let Us Join Our Cheerful Songs

Come, let us join our cheerful songs
With angels round the throne.
Ten thousand thousand are their tongues,
But all their joys are one.

"Worthy the Lamb that died," they cry,
"To be exalted thus."
"Worthy the Lamb," our lips reply,
"For he was slain for us."

"Let all creation join in one
To bless the sacred name
Of him that sits upon the throne
And to adore the Lamb.

PSALM 98

Leader: Shout for joy to the LORD, all the earth,
Children: **Burst into jubilant song with music;**

Leader: Make music to the LORD with the harp,
Children: **With the harp and the sound of singing,**

Leader: With trumpets and the blast of the ram's horn—
Children: **Shout for joy before the LORD, the King.**

PRAYER REQUESTS

THE LORD'S PRAYER *(spoken together)*

OFFERINGS OF LOVE FOR JESUS

Leader: Now, children, go in peace. Live in harmony with one another. Serve the Lord with gladness.

The grace of our Lord ✝ Jesus Christ and the love of God and the fellowship of the Holy Spirit be with you all.

Children: **Amen.**

Rejoice in the Lord Always

Philippians 4:4

Anonymous

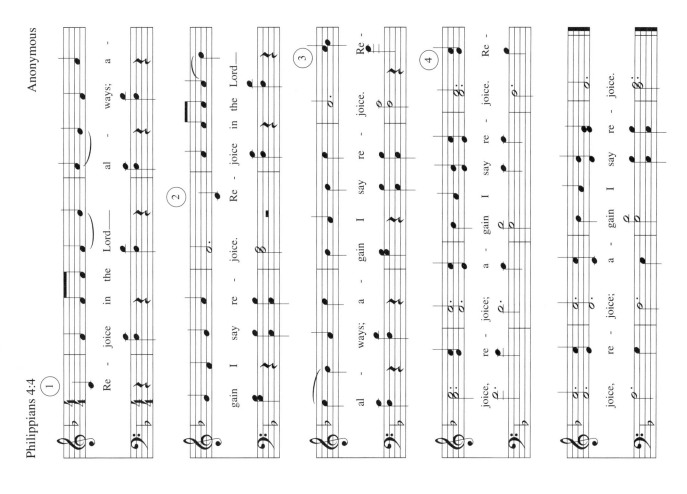

Lord, Open Now My Heart to Hear

Johannes Olearius
tr. Matthias Loy, st. 1,3
Mark A. Jeske, st. 2

Geistliche Lieder zu Wittemberg

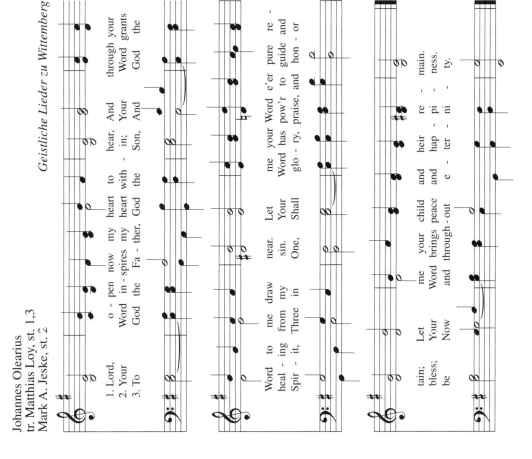

Text tr. st. 2: © 1993 Mark A. Jeske. Used by permission.
Setting: © 1993 Kermit G. Moldenhauer. Used by permission

Praise God, from Whom All Blessings Flow

Thomas Ken

Thomas Tallis

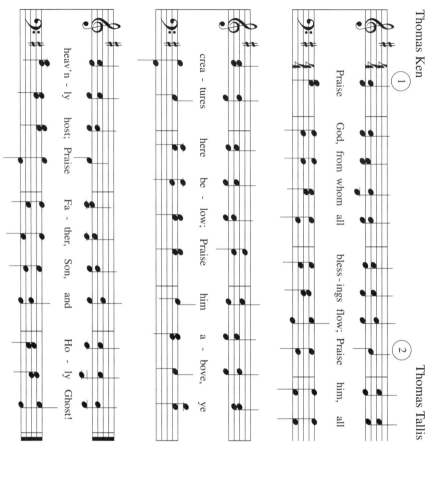

Joy to the World

Isaac Watts

George F. Handel

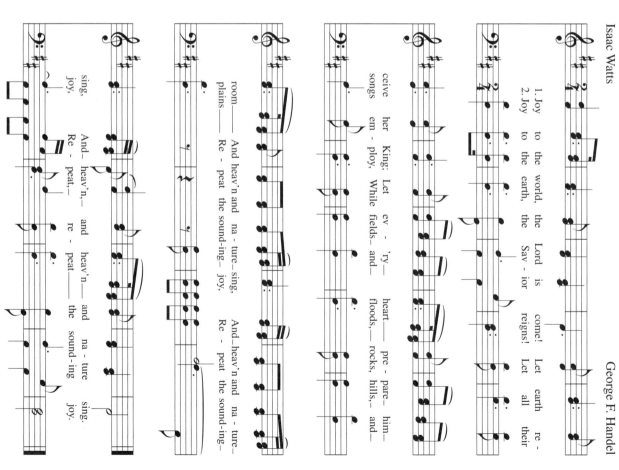

O God from God, O Light from Light

John Julian

Johann Störls . . . Schlag-Gesang-Und Noten-Buch

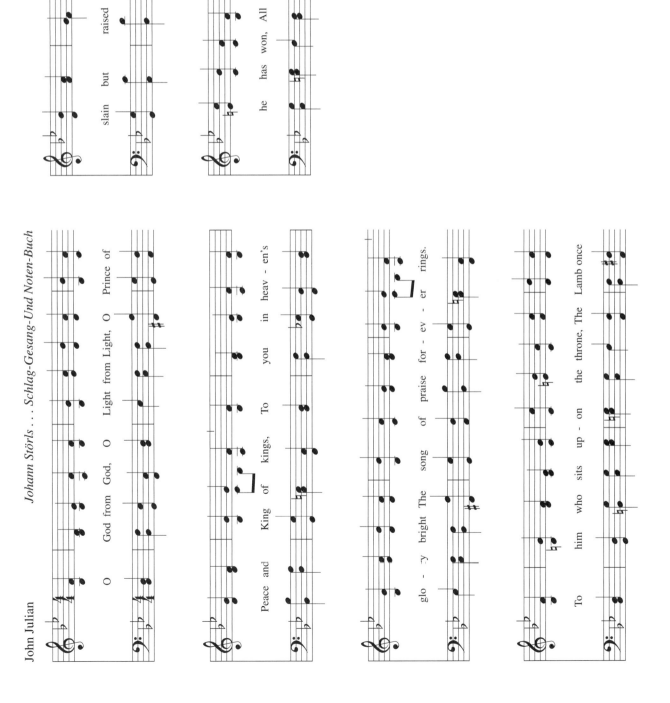

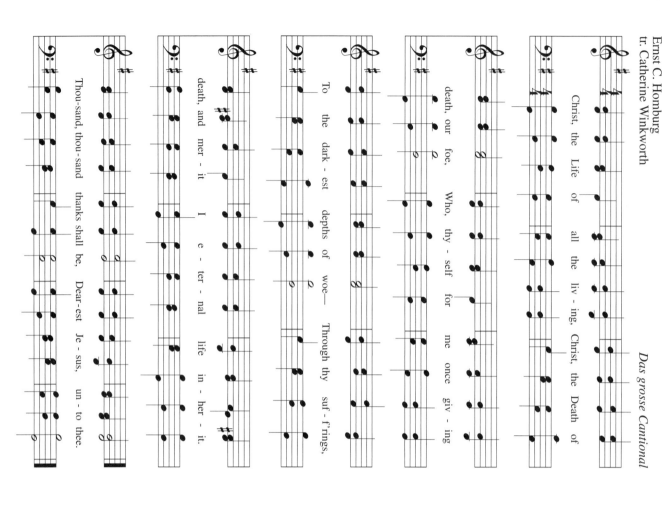

Christ, the Life of All the Living

Ernst C. Homburg
tr. Catherine Winkworth

Das grosse Cantional

Jesus Lives

Joan Eggert

Alleluia! Sing to Jesus

William C. Dix

Ludwig van Beethoven

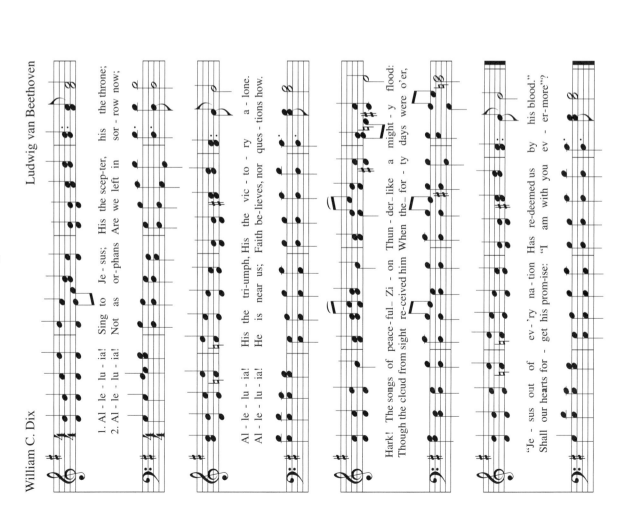